DREAM JOBS IN SPORTS LAW

KATHY FURGANG

ROSEN
PUBLISHING®

New York

Published in 2015 by The Rosen Publishing Group, Inc.
29 East 21st Street, New York, NY 10010

Library of Congress Cataloging-in-Publication Data

Furgang, Kathy, author.
Dream jobs in sports law/Kathy Furgang.
pages cm.—(Great careers in the sports industry)
Includes bibliographical references and index.
ISBN 978-1-4777-7527-1 (library bound)
1. Sports—law and legislation—Vocational guidance—United
States—Juvenile literature. 2. Sports—Vocational guidance—
United States—Juvenile literature. I. Title.
KF299.E57F87 2015
344.73'099—dc23

                                                    2013037046

Manufactured in the United States of America

CONTENTS

Introduction ———————————————— 4

CHAPTER 1 Understanding Sports Law ———————— 8

CHAPTER 2 Getting Prepared for a Career ——————— 21

CHAPTER 3 Jobs at the High School and
College Levels ———————————— 34

CHAPTER 4 The Commissioner's Office ——————— 47

CHAPTER 5 Sports Agents ——————————————— 59

CHAPTER 6 Personal Counsel ———————————— 73

CHAPTER 7 Corporate Attorneys ————————— 86

College and University Programs in
Legal Studies ———————————————— 102

A Career in Sports Law at a Glance ——————— 104

Bureau of Labor Statistics Information ————— 109

Glossary ———————————————————————— 115

For More Information —————————————— 119

For Further Reading —————————————— 123

Bibliography ———————————————————— 125

Index ———————————————————————— 132

INTRODUCTION

The best football players in high schools and colleges can cause a frenzy of attention from recruiters, creating a need for legal advice about the students' future careers.

Imagine a football player who gets plucked from his high school team and showered with attention from recruiters, and then is given offer upon offer to attend colleges with the best football teams in the nation. This is the life of a very few hard-working and talented athletes. When a student is groomed for professional sports, his or her life may change quickly. People in suits grasping briefcases may bombard them, begging to talk with their parents about their bright futures.

The students and families may be excited but also confused and overwhelmed. The number of decisions placed before them may require that a family seek help from professionals who understand how each deal may affect the student's future. Lawyers can help parents and students weed through the offers and the details of the contracts.

A student offered a sports scholarship might be so happy about the offer of money being made that he or she may not fully consider all of the other aspects of the contract. A lawyer that specializes in sports would be an especially valuable person for the family to work with. The lawyer may ask questions that the family has not yet considered. The lawyer could also serve as an in-between contact between the athlete and the school.

As college athletes are recruited for professional teams, the need for a sports lawyer becomes even more necessary. A sports agent is someone who has a specialty in sports law and can help represent the interests of the athlete. For example, where would the athlete live if he had to relocate to another part of the country to be part of a team? What would happen if he were injured on or off the field and unable to play? What would be expected from him in terms of the way he acted off the field? The answers to these questions could lie in the contracts he is being offered. A lawyer could negotiate each term to be something that both parties agree on. Some sports agents stick with the athletes they represent for their entire careers. The lawyer's job is to make his or her client happy and to understand and explain the terms that the athlete will agree to.

Most sports agents and sports lawyers are sports lovers themselves. Some may have been athletes themselves, so they may understand the specific needs of the clients they represent.

The field of sports law is so wide and fascinating that working with individual athletes is only one possibility. Other sports lawyers specialize in working with professional leagues or corporations such as those that make sporting equipment or attire. Other sports lawyers represent athletes in court if they run into legal trouble in their personal or professional lives. Still others work on contracts with the media, sports leagues, or individual teams. The field is fast-paced and requires sharp and personable people who are educated and know the ins and outs of the law. The sports industry is larger than many people imagine, and the need for trained, professional, and knowledgeable lawyers never fades.

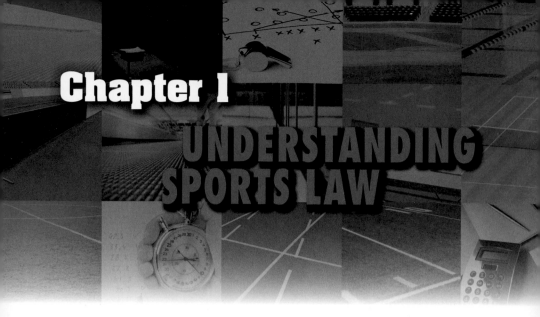

Chapter 1

UNDERSTANDING SPORTS LAW

For someone who loves sports, the game is the most important thing. Many sports lovers remember going to see their first professional game, and they remember the feelings that made them want to continue following their favorite teams or to practice developing their own skills. For some people, that desire for sports lasts well through their adolescent years and into the time they begin thinking about a career.

There have always been many young children who dream of becoming professional athletes and standing before cheering stadium crowds. Then, the dreams begin to fade in later years as the children grow. However, those young children may grow to realize that the sports industry is a wide-open field with endless career opportunities for people off the field and behind the scenes. One branch of the sports industry, sports law, can open many doors for students and provide rewarding and high-paying careers. In order to understand the industry of sports law, here is

Before athletes play their first professional game, they have already negotiated and signed legal contracts with their teams. This is handled, in part, by the agent.

an overview of some different careers in sports law, not all of which require a law degree.

TAKING CARE OF THE ATHLETES

A professional athlete is often highly paid and may switch from team to team over the course of his or her career.

On the day of his retirement from professional baseball in 2013, former New York Yankee Hideki Matsui signs a one-day contract, allowing him to officially retire as a Yankee.

The athlete also depends on his or her body to earn a living. Just one injury could potentially damage the career of an athlete. Because of these unique situations, professional athletes protect themselves by having contracts that lay out specific agreement terms with their employer, or sports team. The details of a contract can become very complex and must take into account certain federal, state,

or even local laws. Someone who knows about law and personal civil rights will be able to help draft, explain, and revise an athlete's contract. Just as the athlete specializes in playing baseball, football, or another sport on the professional level, a contract specialist helps the athlete understand the terms of his or her agreement.

An athlete does not just choose any law specialist to help review a contract and advise whether it should or should not be signed. A professional athlete will choose a trusted representative who can advise him or her in different aspects of the law. The athlete and lawyer may have a long-lasting and trusting relationship that extends through many contracts and personal decisions.

Suppose a professional football player signs a contract that says that he will receive a salary for playing for the team for three years and that he is allowed to endorse products, or star in commercials, for any additional fee given to him from the corporation that makes the product. If the athlete liked working with the lawyer, he may wish to use the lawyer again to help work out a contract for any product endorsement he decides upon in the future. Then the same lawyer could be used again to negotiate the next team contract once the current one expires after the agreed-upon three years. The more work the athlete and lawyer do together, the better their relationship may become. The lawyer becomes familiar with the athlete's history and what kinds of terms are important to him. The lawyer can then better understand in the future what kinds of terms are fair.

For instance, suppose the athlete is injured during his first three-year contract with a team. It helps to have a trusted lawyer who will know the athlete's rights about when he can return to play and how the injury should be able to affect his future contracts. The lawyer is hired by the athlete to keep his or her interests in mind. Lawyers that know the ins and outs of the law will be able to negotiate terms with the sports organization quickly and efficiently so that the athlete is not negatively affected in the future.

The goal of the sports team is to make a profit. The team's management may do this by choosing the best players so they can win the most games and fill the stands. However, their first interest is to make money. A professional team will have its own share of lawyers looking out for the interests of the team. The individual player's lawyer will try to make sure that the player is treated fairly. Both parties understand that professional sports draws interest from fans mainly because of the star power of the athletes. For example, if Peyton Manning can draw thousands of fans to watch Broncos games, buy Broncos memorabilia, and go to stadiums across the country to follow the Denver Broncos, then the star quarterback should be able to draw an excellent salary and benefit in other ways, such as in product endorsements and media appearances.

Members of a team that wins championships and goes to Super Bowls, World Series games, Stanley Cup championships, or NBA play-offs may deserve an extra bonus or consideration when drafting a new contract. The world of negotiations for sports players can be high stakes and difficult. The work of experienced negotiators can help make that work a little easier for the player.

AT THE STADIUM

The world of sports law does not stop at the athlete. The stadiums where the games are played require a considerable amount of work from lawyers to negotiate terms and help make legal decisions. Each stadium is a business unto

itself. There are contracts to be negotiated with concession stand companies, contractors, and security teams.

There are thirty-one stadiums in the United States just to house professional football teams. Add to that the thirty stadiums dedicated to Major League Baseball teams

Each sports stadium in North America represents a number of legal contracts with vendors, including the USTA Billie Jean King National Tennis Center in New York, shown here during the 2013 US Open.

and the stadiums and arenas that are used for basketball, hockey, and soccer games, and there are plenty of opportunities to get involved with sports law. Each stadium is concerned with lawsuits brought on by visitors who might be injured on the property. This means that rules should be put in place to help prevent such injuries. Security crews must be used, safe emergency exits must be provided, and seating and other equipment must be in good working condition. To accomplish all of this, the stadium may need to hire contractors to do the work. Hiring outside contracting companies means drafting contracts and making sure the contractors follow the stadium's rules and guidelines for operating there.

A lawyer's job is not to oversee the whole production but to deal with problems that come up and to understand what is expected of each group as the work is done. In most cases, the lawyer will not be involved after the terms of an agreement are settled—unless something goes wrong. Then the lawyer's knowledge of the law will help the stadium deal with the unexpected. Just as in the case of the lawyer who represents the athlete, the lawyer who represents the stadium will be working with the interest of the stadium in mind.

In addition to making sure the stadium is safe, lawyers may be involved in the agreements between the stadium and companies that sell food or beverages at the concession stands. Companies such as Oscar Meyer, Frito-Lay, Coca-Cola, or Anheuser-Busch must negotiate contracts with every stadium they sell goods to. If a stadium decides to end an agreement with one company and sell a different

KEEP PLAYING BALL

Think about what attracted you to sports as a child. Were you skilled at making baskets in a basketball court in your driveway? Did you look forward to playing catch with your dad in the backyard each summer? Did you love being outside all day biking or playing tennis with your sister? Were you a rising star on your football team? If you can look back and remember what made you passionate about sports in the first place, you may be able to keep that passion through your whole life and career. You may have always dreamed of being a pro ball player but realized life would be better off the courts. There's no reason to stop playing ball. That passion for sports will remain if you continue to play for leisure and fun. A career behind the scenes in sports will bring its own sense of fun and fulfillment. But if you continue to stay involved in sports, you will likely be happy with your chosen career path, even though it is off the playing field.

product, there are often lawyers that get involved in the process. They may negotiate pricing, delivery of goods, and even promotional items and events that take place at the stadium while their products are being sold.

From the payment and vacation time of workers, to the name brands sold at the stadium, to the safety of the locker rooms, bathrooms, and parking lots, there is no lack of opportunity for a lawyer or a lawyer's assistant to get involved.

BACK AT SCHOOL

One of your first memories with organized sports teams may be from a school soccer or baseball team when you were a child. In fact, school sports is one of the most active areas of work in sports law. From elementary school to high school and even to the college level, there are many legal concerns about child and adolescent athletes that must be dealt with carefully.

Most schools, including elementary schools, employ a lawyer who deals with a wide variety of legal issues for the school. While the lawyer must deal with all kinds of legal issues and not specialize in any one area, he or she is faced with many issues of athletics as well. In an elementary school, these issues may be developing school rules that will keep children safe on playing fields and in gym classes. There may be parents who are upset or wish to sue the school because a particular sports team may be open only to a certain gender of student. One legal case in Georgia in 2013 concerned a sixth-grade girl who was allowed to play football on a boys' team, but then the school changed its mind and the girl was removed from the team. The parents sued the school for denying her civil rights to play on a team just like the boys did.

In a lawsuit, the case is discussed in a courtroom and each side defends its own position in the case. A lawyer is the one most familiar with the laws of the institution and the town or state, and with laws regarding citizens' civil rights. One lawyer represents the family, and another one represents the school. If necessary, a school lawyer will go to court to argue a legal case in front of a judge so that a fair decision can be reached.

At the high school level, some athletes are beginning to be recruited by colleges to attend their school after graduation and play on their sports teams. Often there are scholarships involved and contract terms that the student must follow if he or she wishes to take the scholarship and attend the college. Very often, a lawyer may be hired by the family to get involved to help make sure the family and student are treated fairly by the college. The lawyer will help the family understand how the money will be given to the student. The lawyer will also explain what is expected of the student once he or she attends the school in terms of both athletic and academic performance. If the student's contract, or agreement, does not state these things clearly, the lawyer will communicate on behalf of the family to make sure that the issues are stated clearly.

On the college level, lawyers are needed to help families make similar transitions from college play to professional play. Pro teams that try to recruit college players may wish to deal with a lawyer directly, instead of with a family member who may not be familiar with the terms and conditions of the contracts.

The area of sports law can be complex but very rewarding because the lawyer becomes a representative for a hard-working athlete with ambition and hope for an upcoming exciting time in his or her life. Once a lawyer does a job well, his or her client will likely be very pleased and grateful for the help.

DO I HAVE TO GET A LAW DEGREE?

As you will read in the next section, it takes many years of school to become a lawyer. In addition to the schooling, each state has an exam that must be passed by each person who wants to practice law in the state. So, does everyone who works in sports law have to become a lawyer? Absolutely not. There are plenty of jobs in sports law available for people who do not wish to become lawyers. Legal secretaries, paralegals, and law assistants are needed to assist lawyers, and not as much schooling is needed to do these jobs. There are jobs available in the sports industry for people with various levels of law training.

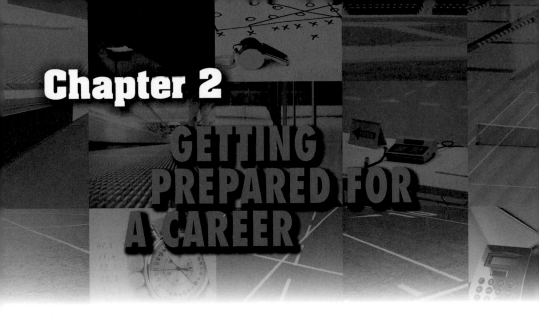

Chapter 2
GETTING PREPARED FOR A CAREER

It might be difficult to know what you want to be when you get old enough to have a career. In fact, you may change your mind several times before you graduate high school. But you will never know what you truly find engaging and fun if you don't do a little research first. Since your interest in sports is likely not going to fade, all you have to do is test your interest in law and figure out if a career in sports law is right for you.

Even if you don't end up going to law school after college, it's never too early to start learning about specializing in the sports field. There are many jobs in the field of sports that do not require a law degree and do not even use law. In fact, a person who becomes a lawyer will have to learn about the entire law profession and then choose a specialty later on. Learning about sports professions can be done without having to go to school. All it takes is a little research and hard work.

READ ALL ABOUT IT

A little research can go a long way for someone who is trying to find his or her way through the sports world. There are plenty of sports publications both in print and online that cover the wide range of jobs available in the sports industry. Your search should go somewhat beyond a subscription to *Sports Illustrated*, however. Look for professional journals that people already working the field might read. These journals can give you a sense of what kinds of jobs are available, what trends exist in the field, and what issues affect the sports business world the most. One popular trade publication for the sports industry is *SportsBusiness Journal*. A daily online version of the publication can be viewed,

as well as an international edition. Another journal, called *Athletic Business*, can help someone just starting out to discover what is interesting about the business.

Read as much as you can about a wide variety of sports. Even though you may wish to work only in the

A student interested in sports law must read as much as possible about the topic and become acquainted with legal issues surrounding many different sports on the professional and college levels.

world of Major League Baseball, you should have a wide range of knowledge about different sports. The sports periodicals can help give you that well-rounded knowledge of hiking, biking, or even Little League or car racing. In addition to having diverse knowledge, you are also helping yourself prepare for a career you may not know you will have in the future. Even though you may wish to work only in baseball, you may not be able to find a job in that field. Having read a lot about different kinds of sports, your options would still be open in different fields. Read about player contracts to see the going rates for athletes in different sports. Read about what kinds of agreements athletes make with private corporations to be spokespeople for their products.

Major newspapers such as the *Wall Street Journal*, the *New York Times*, and *Newsday* also have in-depth sports sections that discuss a wide variety of topics about the industry. The more you research, the more you will learn.

VOLUNTEER YOUR TIME

While it may be too early to get a paying job in the sports industry, it may not be too early to volunteer your time or become an intern for a company that helps to train young people. Any experience, from interning for a local college team to volunteering at a summer sports camp, can

Volunteering or coaching is a great way to get involved in the sports industry on a local level and gain experience to put on your résumé.

give you an idea about what kinds of issues come up in a sports-related field. It will be unlikely that volunteer jobs for high school students will be directly related to the field of sports and law, but the experience can help you learn about the jobs that people have and the kinds of duties they are responsible for.

Check local newspapers or online sources to find out what companies might be looking for help. You may not even see an advertisement for a volunteer job opening or internship. If there is a particular sports team near your home that you are interested in getting to know more about, you can call them to ask about possible volunteer opportunities. Getting help or advice from a parent or gym teacher at school can also be a good idea. He or she may be able to make you aware of jobs you had not considered or that you never knew existed.

Make sure that you ask a lot of questions, no matter what kind of volunteer job or internship you get. Find out how much education people have and whether their education is related to sports or law in particular. Spread the word that you may be interested in a career in the sports industry and that you want to learn as much as you can. Keep your eyes and ears open. You may be surprised about what information people can offer. Ask specifically about the legal side of the business. If you are lucky enough to work around a lawyer, be respectful of how often you interact with that person or ask questions. Make sure the person is friendly, approachable, and interested in interacting with young people in a mentoring capacity.

REQUEST AN INFORMATIONAL INTERVIEW

Remember that if you have an internship or volunteer position in an office environment, there are rules of etiquette to follow. Interrupting a person in his or her office is usually frowned upon. Work with a supervisor or adviser if you can to arrange an informational interview or an informal time for you to speak with a professional about his or her experiences and background. Lawyers may have especially tight schedules during the workday, so arranging for a convenient time to speak will benefit both you and the lawyer. This may end up helping you in the long run because your interview subject will be more prepared to speak with you.

Look for the person at your job who might be most involved in law. For example, if you volunteer at a local college athletics department, you may wish to arrange an informational interview with the person who has the title of compliance officer. A compliance officer is someone who is responsible for knowing and enforcing the rules of the NCAA, or National Collegiate Athletic Association. While the person may not be a lawyer, he or she will understand the importance of the school and its student athletes following

Arranging for an informational interview with a lawyer or someone in a law office can make your job or internship especially valuable.

the rules set out for them by the association. A school that does not follow the rules of the NCAA can lose its ability to play as a Division I, Division II, or Division III school. These are the divisions set up so that schools can compete against each other on equal footing and ensure fair play. This includes certain academic standards student athletes must meet. An informational interview with a compliance officer can help you discover whether you enjoy the legal aspect of the industry and wish to continue pursuing it. The officer may also be able to give advice about schools or programs near you that can help you prepare for a career in sports law.

INTERVIEW TIPS

The interview process is an important part of the experience that any young person goes through to get a paying job, a volunteer job, or an internship. An interview can be nerve-wracking for anyone looking for a job, but young people have less experience. They may benefit from keeping certain things in mind. Remember that the person you are talking to is older and has experience in the industry. Always be polite and respectful, giving answers in a courteous way. Wear clothes that are as businesslike as possible. If you have a suit or business dress, wear it to the interview. Even though the sports industry is a notoriously casual business in which people wear athletic clothing, employees do not wear this kind of clothing in offices. Most offices maintain a professional atmosphere, and you should try to look as professional as possible.

DO YOUR RESEARCH

Even for the most dedicated high school student, a law degree, or Juris Doctor (JD), is many years away. But remember that becoming a lawyer is not your only option. Find out ahead of time what kind of education and training is required for each level of legal study.

To become a lawyer, a person first needs to obtain an undergraduate, or bachelor's, degree. Then, an exam called the LSAT is required for admission into law schools in the United States, Canada, and some other countries.

Similar to admission to an undergraduate college, the law school will consider your grades and LSAT scores before admitting you to its JD program. A JD program is usually a three-year, full-time program. Students will gain a general understanding of law, and many law schools allow students to also major, or specialize, in a particular area of law. Sports law is included as a specialization of law, so students looking at law schools should consider the quality of the school's sports law program.

Upon graduation, the student will take a state test, called a bar examination, to become eligible to practice law in a particular state. The state that your law school was in does not affect the bar exam you will take. For example, if you go to law school in Connecticut but plan to practice law in New York, you would take the bar exam for the state of New York. Some students take several bar exams to allow them to study law in different states or to improve their options for where they can apply for jobs.

The academic demands of law school are very rigorous, and the schools and exams can be quite costly. Most lawyers feel the effort and time is worth it because lawyers can command high salaries when they finally begin practicing law.

There are many other options besides going to law school and taking a bar exam. Earning a legal secretary certificate is the fastest way to begin working in the field of law. The course teaches about effective communication,

A legal secretary certificate is one option for someone interested in sports law, and a degree in paralegal studies is also an option for people not interested in pursuing a Juris Doctor degree.

ethical decision making, critical thinking, and other common law theories and practices. Online courses are also available for people interested in earning the certificate.

Another option for education in the legal world is either an associate's degree or a bachelor's degree in

CHOOSING THE RIGHT SCHOOL

The search for a college that's right for you can be a difficult task. But if you break the job down into smaller tasks, it will be manageable and possible for you. First, make lists of what kinds of courses you are looking for in a school. Think about the school size and location that might interest you most. Then check libraries or online sources for resources that provide this information. Guides by publishers such as Barron's and Peterson's have been the leading sources of college data for decades. The guides allow you to search schools by academic level, size, course offerings, price, location, or other searchable features. Even though a law degree is a postgraduate degree, you may want to know what undergraduate schools have courses that teach about law to those who may be interested in it. And don't forget online courses. Some online degrees may allow students to specialize in areas such as law or sports.

paralegal studies. An associate's degree is generally a two-year program, while a bachelor's degree is a four-year program. A paralegal aids lawyers in a law office and can get a lot of hands-on experience working with clients and learning about law. Paralegals assist clients, perform legal research, communicate with clients, prepare legal documents, and assist lawyers in preparing for courtroom cases.

Another option for someone who does not have a Juris Doctor degree is to get a bachelor's degree or a master's degree in legal studies. Many of the topics taught in a legal studies program are taught in law school, and some people who take the bachelor's degree program may choose to go on to attend a Juris Doctor program. The legal studies degree is also a good option for someone who has earned an associate's degree, such as in paralegal studies, and wishes to continue his or her education.

The options for getting a law education are so varied because educators as well as employers know that the commitment to going to law school and knowing that you want to become a lawyer when you have only just finished high school is a difficult decision. Many people try other educational options first and then eventually decide to go to law school after a few years of working in the field. There are plenty of educational options open for people interested in law, and the outlook for jobs in this field tends to be high.

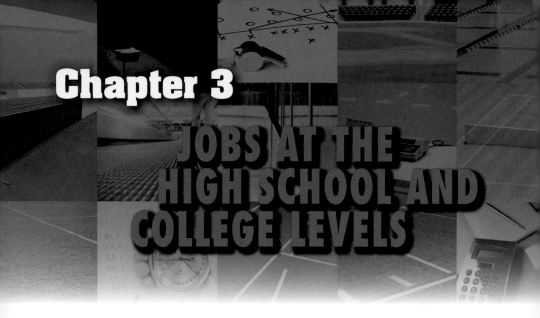

Chapter 3

JOBS AT THE HIGH SCHOOL AND COLLEGE LEVELS

Many of the people who get the most hands-on experience in sports law work in high schools and colleges. There are general guidelines for high schools to follow so that their programs treat students fairly and ensure that coaches are acting properly as they do their jobs. The National Federation of State High School Associations (NFHS) helps establish rules for competition and oversees unique issues that come up in different sports that schools might not be able to handle themselves.

In addition to the National Federation of State High School Associations, most states have their own organizations that guide school districts on how to structure and carry out their athletics programs. At the state level, organizations might monitor the way coaches interact with athletes, ensuring that they treat athletes fairly and that they keep athletes as safe and protected as possible. In the event of student injuries, the responsibility of the coach

Athlete injuries are one of the biggest legal concerns for high schools and colleges with sports programs. They must look out for the welfare of the players.

may be assessed to make sure that the coach or school was not to blame for the student's injuries.

School districts work most closely with students and families in cases of disagreements and legal issues, and the higher levels get involved as needed.

One of the most common sources of lawsuits is a violation of Title IX. This is a document that is part of the 1972 Education Amendments put out by the U.S. Department of Labor. The amendment states that there should be no discrimination in sports based on the sex of the athlete. In many cases, that means that schools must provide specific sports teams for both boys and girls, or they must allow the teams to be coed, meaning that they include both male and female athletes. The amendment is detailed as to what is and is not included in the Title IX agreement, so lawyers are often needed to interpret the document in relation to a specific legal case.

For example, a fourteen-year-old Indiana girl, Logan Young, sued the Indiana High School Athletic Association as well as the Monroe County Community School

Corporation for allegedly violating Title IX and not allowing her to try out for and play on her high school's baseball team. She did not wish to play on the softball

One of the most important jobs a sports lawyer has is explaining contracts and other legal details to the client he or she represents.

team, knowing that the rules and competition were different from those of baseball. Her family hired a lawyer to represent her. According to her statement, she was not given the same opportunities as boys who played baseball. The statement said, "Logan will be irreparably harmed by losing the chance to play baseball with her peers and to develop skills to enable her to progress to the next level of baseball; Logan will be irreparably harmed by being denied other tangible and intangible benefits of baseball participation made available to similarly situated boys. Having an opportunity to play softball will not adequately compensate Logan for losing the opportunity to play baseball, and will place her at a substantial disadvantage compared to her peers who played baseball." As a result of the lawsuit, the athletic association adopted an emergency rule that permits girls to try out for their high school baseball teams.

In another case of a lawsuit involving high school sports, a New Jersey public school football coach was sued for bowing and kneeling in prayer with his football team before games. His actions, it was decided by a court, violated the nation's clear separation of church and state. The president of the town's board of education stated, "Public school officials simply may not engage with students in religious activity. The board of education and district officials have, throughout this case, made certain no school employee supervises or otherwise participates in any type of prayer with our students. Needless to say, the board is pleased that, in this case, the courts reaffirmed this long-standing constitutional principle."

There are many other examples of times that high school or even elementary school sports can lead to legal issues. In some cases, homeschooled students may decide that they wish to take part in team sports in public schools, even though they are not enrolled in those schools. Laws differ by state as to whether these students have a right to participate in a team sport without being a student at the school. In other cases, a student might be injured on school grounds during a sports game or practice. A student from another school may be injured at an away game at a school he or she does not attend. Any lawsuits that arise from these kinds of situations can be tricky and need to be handled by experienced lawyers who are familiar with the law.

OFF TO COLLEGE

Sports lawyers may also be necessary when colleges recruit high school athletes. The recruiters often offer scholarships to the athletes in hopes that they will attend the college and play for their team. The scholarship may come with legal agreements that the student must abide by in order to get the scholarship money. That may mean keeping up a certain grade point average during each year of college or

DIVISIONS OF THE NCAA

The National Collegiate Athletic Association (NCAA) has divided its members into different divisions so that similar schools can compete against each other fairly. Here is a basic description of the three divisions.

Division I These colleges and universities are often the largest in the country. There is a lot of competition among athletes on Division I teams, and the scholarship opportunities are the greatest in this division. Professional teams often scout Division I teams for athletes to join them after graduation.

Division II These colleges and universities are smaller than Division I schools, and there is much less opportunity for scholarships here. In fact, there is a limit to the amount of financial aid that teams can receive. The athletics programs must be financed through the college's budget, just like other academic departments at the school. Each Division II school must offer at least five sports for women and five for men, including two team sports for both women and men.

Division III These colleges offer no athletic scholarships at all and no financial aid to teams outside the department budget. Not a lot of recruiting happens at this level, and there is less competition among athletes. The schools in this division must offer at least five sports for women and five for men.

dedicating a certain number of hours to team practice or play, or it may mean that a certain behavioral code must be followed. All of these conditions should be reviewed by adult family members who feel they understand what is being asked. It is often wise for families to have the conditions reviewed by a lawyer to make sure everyone feels the student can live up to the school's expectations. The loss of scholarship money can devastate a family, as well as interfere with the student's chance of getting a college education. If there is something the college is requesting of the student that the family thinks is unreasonable or might cause the student difficulties, a lawyer may be able to work out another agreement with the school.

While it is true that the services of a lawyer will cost the family money, they will likely benefit from the lawyer's services and end up saving money in the end by getting the best scholarship agreement they can for their child. In addition, a family who does not have a lawyer review agreements may not be aware of whether all of the conditions placed on the student are customary or fair.

THE NCAA

Once a student athlete has made it to the college level, there is a whole new set of rules and regulations to keep athletes, coaches, and lawyers on their toes. The National Collegiate Athletic Association (NCAA) is a group that organizes the athletics programs of many of the colleges and universities in the United States and Canada. The NCAA puts forth rules for each of the collegiate games and has panels that approve any changes to the games. It has divided the colleges into three main divisions and has rules that colleges must follow in order to be considered part of each division. Some of the rules involve school size, the number of sports offered at the school, and athlete academic achievement.

If student athletes or school coaches and officials do not follow the rules set out by the NCAA for their division of play, they may face consequences. Athletes who do not follow the rules may be suspended from play. There may be more serious consequences, such as fines for the school to pay or even the loss of eligibility for the school to compete as part of its assigned division.

COMPLIANCE OFFICERS

The NCAA rulebook is over four hundred pages long, which means sports law at the college level can be particularly complicated. The person who would interact most with and be most familiar with the NCAA rules is a compliance officer working at a college or university. This person may have a background in law, but it is not required that the person have a law degree. Most have college degrees and may get extra training while on the job.

SPOTTING TALENT

University compliance officers are often on the lookout for violations of Division I recruiting regulations. Division I sports is big business, partly because of the money that is allowed from corporate and commercial sponsors who support the televised games and attract fans to the stands. Division I schools know that their athletes may soon become professional athletes after graduation, so they choose the recruits carefully from high schools around the nation. Schools compete for the best athletes, and there is always a chance for unethical behavior or bribes to get the students they want for their teams. That's why it is important for compliance officers to make sure that the act of spotting and recruiting talent for their teams remains lawful and within the regulations of the NCAA.

Compliance officers work in many different fields. Factories, industrial plants, government agencies, and large facilities all use compliance officers to make sure rules are followed and a safe working environment is maintained. The job of each compliance officer differs based on the field that the person works in. Naturally, a compliance officer who works in an athletics department at a college or university will need knowledge of sports as well as a dedication to understanding the complex regulations of the NCAA. In addition, the compliance officer should have an ability to interact with students, coaches, and parents when the situation arises. Sometimes student athletes do not know that they have violated an NCAA rule until they are alerted by either a compliance officer or coach.

Many of the rules that students, and sometimes coaches, are not aware of have to do with accepting bribes. For example, there are some cases in which a complimentary meal for an athlete might be considered a bribe, or an illegal gift. Student athletes are not allowed to borrow money from some people, such as coaches or

referees. There are even rules about who should receive frequent flier miles when an athlete travels by air on a ticket paid for by the university.

The growing use of technology and social networking has brought about new rules concerning how recruiters and coaches are allowed to communicate with athletes

The rules of the NCAA are especially complicated in terms of player conduct. It is very important for both the coaches and players to understand all of the rules that apply to the athletes in their division.

through texting, e-mailing, and social networking sites such as Facebook. It is the compliance officer's job to understand the regulations and to understand when they are being violated.

The officer cannot keep track of every athlete's actions, but in cases where complaints are made about the questionable actions of coaches or athletes, the compliance officer should be able to identify whether the situation violates any of the rules for the institution's division status.

A compliance officer may have to analyze each situation individually and request legal advice when needed. There are many innocent violations of rules that occur accidentally. The student or coach may innocently accept a gift from someone and not realize that it might be considered a bribe. A coach may communicate with a potential recruit by text but not realize that the form of communication is not allowed.

Students in college athletics may be surprised by the large number of regulations and restrictions on their actions. The job of the compliance officer is to make sure that students understand their roles as school athletes and have honest interactions with each other and with coaches that will not harm the school's position in its division.

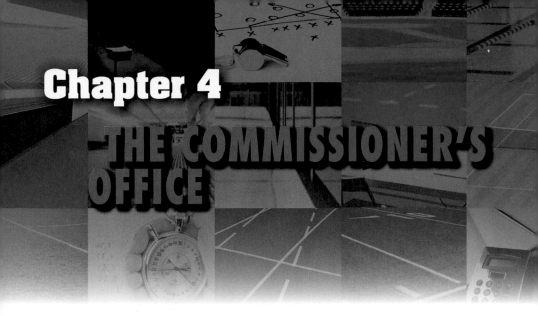

Chapter 4
THE COMMISSIONER'S OFFICE

T he professional world of sports is the ultimate goal of most dedicated athletes. After spending their whole lives watching their favorite teams and admiring pro players, making it into the pro leagues is the ultimate success story. Millions of people watch professional games every season. Just the Super Bowl or the World Series is enough to have millions of people tuning into prime time television every year. The amount of support behind pro sports makes it a big business, complete with powerful corporate sponsors that spend millions of dollars on commercials, billboards at games, and endorsements with athletes to promote their products. Many athletes in professional football, basketball, and baseball command salaries in the millions of dollars.

With so much at stake in the world of pro sports, it's no wonder that some oversight is needed to make sure that corruption does not take over the honest pursuit of the game. The stakes are higher, and the potential for corruption is even higher, at the professional level than at the college level. An office is appointed to regulate each sport to make sure that rules are followed and corruption does not occur. This office is called the commissioner's office. A baseball commissioner, a football commissioner, and a basketball commissioner are appointed and lead a team of people who regulate and enforce the laws of the sport. The commissioners themselves command salaries in the millions, and they have a greater influence in their field than any other person, including star athletes. The

behind-the-scenes decisions that are made by sports

commissioners affect the fans, the athletes, and the sport itself. It is without a doubt one of the most difficult jobs in the field of sports. Here are a few of the

The locations of some professional championship games, such as Super Bowl XLVII played in New Orleans in 2013, are contracted years in advance.

jobs that the commissioner will be responsible for in each sport.

SETTING RULES

In order to be part of any professional sports organization, it is important that firm rules are set so that all of the people involved know what is expected of them. Rules set up by the commissioner's office provide consistency across all teams so that play is fair and consistent. For example, rules set up for safety in the NFL must be set for all teams or some will be at a disadvantage when on the field. Rules applied to umpires, referees, coaches, or other employees needed in the game must be consistent across all teams. When large amounts of money are at stake in professional games, the rules become especially important. Any question about what type of play is allowed on the field can escalate into an argument among players or referees and may potentially affect the outcome of the game. When rules are firm and easily understood, everyone involved has a better experience with the game.

The rules include everything from when a team can forfeit a game, the parameters for deciding events such as overtime, coin tosses, and when player substitutions can and should be used. The rules do more than just keep the game running smoothly. Another reason the rules are so important is potential lawsuits might involve rules that are thought to have been broken by one party or another. For example, if an injury occurs, a player may be at fault for unnecessary roughness as defined in the rulebooks. Much like the laws of a city or town, the rules of a professional sports league keep games orderly following a consistent practice or protocol.

ENFORCING RULES

One of the main ways that rules are enforced in professional sports is by placing a fine on players who disobey the rules. In the 2012 NFL season, there were 164 incidences that resulted in fines for players, totaling $2,873,075 for the season. Many of them were instances of fighting, hitting, kicking, or unnecessary roughness against other players. The fines increase with the severity of the offense. Other lesser offenses include violations of uniform regulation or wearing messages on uniforms to promote a company or product.

With enough fines and violations, a team may be at risk of being removed from the game, although offenses rarely become that frequent or severe.

Although there are long rulebooks with minute details about the rules of each professional sport, that does not mean the rules are always enforced and punishments are handed out to offenders. There are often rules that referees let slide because they don't seem to hurt the game either way. However, when rules are abused, there may be an increase in penalties. For example, in the 2013 season, the National Football League was expected to tighten its enforcement of rules that prohibit coaches from stepping out onto the playing field during games. There will be more warning to coaches that stepping out onto the field is an intimidating interference and will be met with penalties in the future, and the penalties may affect the team in the long run. The rule was overlooked in the past because it was not frequently violated. However, an increase in violations has brought it to the attention of the league and its referees.

NFL rules attempt to keep the disruptions of coaches and referees to a minimum, and fines may be given out for breaking the rules. Here, Washington Redskins coach Mike Shanahan argues with a referee.

OVERSEEING CONTRACTS

The contracts of professional athletes are what keep the games going and what keeps the athletes satisfied with their work. Without a contract, the athlete is unsure about his or her future in the sport. Will this be the last season with this team? What will my pay be next season? Will I be expected to attend promotional events? If so, how many? The athlete's contract answers all of these questions and allows the athlete to concentrate on his or her game and performance. The commissioner oversees all of these negotiations and contracts, but things don't always go as smoothly as expected. In the 2012–2013 professional hockey season, there was a player lockout. The players wanted to be able to have more say in the terms of their contracts and more leverage in being able to negotiate their contracts. By refusing to attend practices, the players sent a strong message to the commissioner that changes needed to be made. National Hockey League (NHL) commissioner Gary Bettman and deputy commissioner Bill Daly met with a lawyer, Scot Beckenbaugh, who specializes in mediation, or intervening between people in disputes in order to bring about an agreement. After a 113-day lockout, an agreement was finally reached and the season began. The lockout came close to threatening the entire season, which it did in the 2004–2005 season. If

COMMISSIONERS ON EVERY LEVEL

There are commissioners in all levels of sports, not just in the professional leagues. Every organization in sports, from recreation commissions to colleges and universities may have a person in the role of commissioner. This person may work with budgets, make and agree upon registration costs, oversee registration, attend meetings and represent the league in broader meetings such as town meetings or university meetings, oversee the inventory of uniforms and equipment, and deal with the disciplinary issues of players and coaches. People in the position of commissioner in minor or nonprofessional leagues are not likely to be practicing lawyers. Regardless of their degree, commissioners at any level need to understand the law that governs the sport and the issues that may affect the players, coaches, and fans.

that had occurred, employees would have been terminated and the entire league would have faced the possibility of bankruptcy. The job of the commissioner is especially important in situations like these, and there is no one higher than the commissioner who can negotiate or provide players with what they need to continue the game.

Similarly, there was an NFL referee lockout at the beginning of the 2012 football season. In that case, NFL commissioner Roger Goodell was in the position to negotiate a settlement that caused the referees to be able to return to work. In the meantime, however, the interruption to the NFL season was difficult for players and fans as well. Fill-in referees were put into the games, and some of their calls were seriously questioned. Fans and players were eager for the dispute to be worked out and the season to return to normal. Lawyers on both sides of the debate worked hard to end the problem and keep the permanent, experienced referees working.

MAKING DEALS

Another thing that falls upon the responsibility of the commissioner's office is the way deals are made with outside parties such as broadcasters and advertisers. These contracts are worth millions of dollars each season, and they affect the way people view and perceive the games. The advertising used in stadiums as well as during commercial television breaks must be negotiated with the sports organizations. The television stations that will broadcast the games must make a deal with the commissioner's office.

One of the biggest sports event moneymakers worldwide is the soccer World Cup. ESPN pays about $100 million for the right to broadcast the games in the English language, while Spanish broadcasting company Univision pays about $325 million for broadcasting rights around the world.

SETTING THE TONE

Not every task a sports commissioner has is included in the job description. One unspoken part of the commissioner's job is to instill a good attitude among the players, coaches, and fans. Rules that are unreasonably strict or forget the lighthearted aspects of the game will lower the morale of the game. This can be true among players as well as among fans. For example, in an effort to keep a baseball stadium clean, a commissioner may decide that peanuts and popcorn should no longer be sold in the stadium. While that would certainly cut down on messes, most fans would be upset by that sudden restriction and may not feel that the stadium appreciates their business. After all, the fans are the ones who bring money into the stadium, fill the stands, and provide encouragement to the team. A better decision by the commissioner would be to increase the number of cleanup crews during the game so that spilled popcorn or peanut shells can be cleaned up as the game progresses, instead of waiting until after the stadium empties out. The decisions the commissioner makes can affect the mood and tone of the entire sports experience.

Think about all of the money brought in each year by play-off games and the Super Bowl. The Nielson Research Group, the company that tracks television ratings in the United States, reports that ten of the most watched television

The World Cup soccer finals are one of the most popular and lucrative sports events in the world. Media outlets negotiate for the rights to broadcast the games.

events of all time include four Super Bowl games. That means that contracts to broadcast professional football are extremely lucrative and very big business. The NFL creates contracts with every major television company, as well as satellite radio and other media outlets, such as Yahoo!

HAVING INFLUENCE

Sports commissioners are the most powerful and influential people in professional sports. In addition to NFL commissioner Roger Goodell, there are other influential commissioners, such as Major League Baseball commissioner Bud Selig and National Basketball Association commissioner David Stern. The decisions these commissioners make affect many people, which is why their decisions may not always be popular with fans or players. The commissioners themselves are all lawyers, but there are many people who work in the commissioner's office who do not have a legal degree. These people do a lot of behind-the-scenes work that helps the commissioner make decisions and structure the games. The employees in the commissioner's office may specialize in marketing, business, or public relations, or they may be paralegals who understand the business of law but do not have a degree to practice law. There may also be many other lawyers who help negotiate contracts and arbitrate, or settle, disputes. They may be there to help when players are traded, or they may help decide what to do if a player is involved in a legal matter in his or her personal life. The legal specialists help keep the game running smoothly and profitably.

Chapter 5

SPORTS AGENTS

While a recruiter may be the person who spots talent in high schools and colleges around the country, it is the sports agent who can make that person's career take off and even skyrocket to fame. The job of a sports agent is perhaps one of the most desired behind-the-scenes jobs in the field of sports, and it is certainly the most sought-after one in the field of sports law.

It is not required that a sports agent have a law degree. However, the most competitive and professional agents do have a Juris Doctor degree and are certified to practice the law. The best agents have strong personalities that are outgoing and friendly, and they can be downright aggressive at times. Their job is to represent their client and to get the best possible deal for the client.

It is not only the superstar athletes with the highest salaries and the biggest product promotions who need an agent to represent them and look out for their best interest. Any professional athlete would be advised to have an agent to review contract terms and negotiate contracts with them. The reason is that the stakes are high. Consider the average salary of athletes in the four major American sports leagues—basketball, baseball, football, and hockey. The average professional salary that athletes in any of these sports makes in one season is more than the average American will make in a lifetime of working. However, keep in mind that the average pro athlete's career is about four years long.

An agent who is experienced in negotiating salaries not only can get a client more money than the client may be able to get on his or her own but is also familiar with the going rates of the athlete's peers. The agent knows how many years is reasonable for a player to be contracted with a team and when it is appropriate to negotiate a better contract. A lot of this knowledge comes with experience on the job and not education or time spent in law school. However, knowledge of the law, especially contract law, will greatly increase an agent's value to the client.

Just as with a professional league's commissioner's office, an agent's office may be filled with people who

Sports agent Scott Boras talks with Adrian Beltre in 2009, when he played for the Seattle Mariners. Boras represents several professional athletes.

do different tasks for the agency, while having different levels of education. Here are some of the duties of an agent's office, whether the work is done directly by the agent or by other support staff.

NEGOTIATING CONTRACTS

The work of negotiating with a sports team about an athlete's salary and contract is most often done by the agent directly. It is probably the most difficult work and requires vast knowledge of the law, sports, trends in the business, and the athlete's needs and wants. The agent must be reasonable with both parties in consideration. Most athletes on team sports have a contract that keeps them on that team for a given amount of time, such as a few seasons at a time. The contract lasts for that period of time, guaranteeing a salary for each year or for the time period. On average, athletes in the NBA fetch the highest salaries, at an average of $5.15 million per season. The agent would know this when negotiating salaries, and the agent would also know the reason why. There are far fewer athletes in professional basketball than any of the other three main professional sports—baseball, football, or hockey.

An NBA team has a maximum of fifteen players on each team. There are thirty NBA teams, so that's a total of 450 NBA players at any one time. Compare that to football, which has the lowest average yearly salary. Even though football brings in more money through advertising and broadcasting revenue, the average player salary is $1.9 million. That's because each team has a total of fifty-three players, and there are thirty-two NFL teams.

That means there is a total of 1,696 players in a season of football. Even with more money being generated for the league than basketball, the money must be spread among nearly four times as many players.

It's true that average salaries represent just that—averages. There are pro athletes who get much more and much less each year. Agents are aware of salary caps and salary minimums as well as the public perception of high

Professional basketball players get the highest average salaries in professional sports, due to the fact that there are fewer players and teams in basketball than there are in professional football.

salaries and the players who receive them. If an agent thinks his or her client is worth a lot more than he is being paid, high-stakes negotiations will take place so that that athlete will be satisfied. Athletes who feel they are well respected by their team's owners, not just their fan base, will likely perform better and contribute to the team in a more positive way.

Sometimes negotiating product deals can help a player command a higher salary from the team he plays for. For example, if a player gets endorsements from the athletic company Nike and begins being featured in Nike advertisements, the player's fan base will likely increase because of the public exposure. This may get more fans into the stadium or to tune in on television. As a result, the team owners and managers may take notice. Their player has suddenly increased in value for the team, allowing a higher salary or a better contract to be negotiated.

When teams search around before each season look-ing for replacement players, draft picks, or high-profile trades, they often approach the agent instead of going directly to the athlete. The agent is the business face for the player, almost treating the player as a valuable busi-ness unto himself. The agent may consider the offer of the other team and negotiate for more money and better terms before even approaching the athlete with the idea. Then further negotiations may be considered, such as any relocating fees for the athlete's family or smaller perks that might sweeten the deal for the athlete.

ADVISING CLIENTS

When it comes to providing legal advice to an athlete, or any kind of professional advice for that matter, the agent may be the person in the best position to do so. An agent who works with many athletes has a broad understanding of many teams and how each might interact with and treat its players. This kind of advice might be extremely valuable to someone who is considering an offer from another team. The experiences of the agent's other clients can provide a wealth of information for the agent to pass on to others. Any team that might have a reputation for mistreating athletes or going back on its word in negotiations will have difficulties shaking that reputation when it must deal with the same agents representing multiple clients. If an athlete has a good and stable deal with a respectable team with a good record, the agent may advise the client to stay with that team and negotiate a higher salary under the same terms rather than relocate to a new team with a reputation that is in question.

An agent may also be in a good position to negotiate smaller parts of a contract that the athlete may not think of. Each team deals with injured athletes differently. Some have a pool of money that they use to help athletes and their families through difficult times of injury and lost work. Comparing each team and its policy on this is wise when considering which team to play for. Some athletes feel the compensation and the coverage provided to professional athletes has been decreasing over the years, and the issue is becoming more important. Professional football players Tom Brady and Drew Brees have brought the public's attention to a proposed bill in California that would limit professional athletes' ability to file a claim with a court to be compensated for care they need for on-the-job injuries. That's why it is especially important for athletes and agents to negotiate good contracts that explain how the athlete will be treated in the event of an injury that makes the athlete unable to play.

ACCOUNTING AND LEGAL DUTIES

The more clients a sports agent works with, the more legal and accounting paperwork the agency will have to deal with. For example, copies of every legal document about any negotiations or communication must be kept on file. A support staff often does this work, as well as keeping track of salary histories for each player and the dates of each contract.

The paperwork in a sports agent's office should be able to be accessed quickly and accurately at a moment's notice, in case an emergency situation arises with the client or sports team. The support staff will often keep these

SHOW ME THE MONEY!

The 1996 film *Jerry Maguire*, starring Tom Cruise and Cuba Gooding Jr., is about a once big-time sports agent who is struggling to maintain his career while representing a loyal but demanding football player as a client. The fast-paced and high-stakes atmosphere of the business is showcased, as well as the importance of producing the bottom line of the sports business—money. The movie features a hilarious scene in which Gooding's character, Rod Tidwell, gets his agent to identify with his perspective of the agent/athlete relationship by making Cruise's character, Jerry Maguire, repeatedly scream over the phone, "Show me the money!" In addition to the characters' quest for cash and success, the film also shows the importance of trust in the client and agent relationship.

files and documents organized and then are able to assist the agent in finding and using the files.

Paralegals might be used in this capacity, or legal secretaries who have knowledge of sports teams or athletes. Paralegals typically have a bachelor's degree, while legal secretaries may have an associate's degree or certification.

A sport agent's office may also employ people with no particular training in law or in sports. People without specialty degrees can do many of the jobs that are needed to make an office run smoothly. On-the-job training is an important aspect of the sports industry, no matter what your education level. Showing an interest in sports is a good way to get your foot in the door at a sports agent's office. Understanding the parts of the contracts will come with time, but an interest in and a love of sports comes naturally to some people more than others. If you are someone with a love of sports, you may be able to handle the day-to-day duties of an agent's office without legal training. Accounting and legal departments are just a couple of areas in which people without specialty degrees may learn on the job with help from supervisors and managers.

MARKETING CLIENTS

The negotiation of an athlete's team contract is not the only duty an agent has for his or her client. Athletes are big business for companies that do advertising and products that want star endorsements. From sneakers to

Many professional athletes supplement their salaries by negotiating product endorsements with sporting companies such as Nike, Adidas, Reebok, and others.

sporting equipment to cars and breakfast cereals, there are endless opportunities for athletes to cash in on advertising. The opportunities give the athletes incredible exposure to sports fans, and even to people who aren't regular sports fans. When athletes appear in prime-time advertising or magazine or newspaper ads, the general public becomes familiar with them, not just the fans of their particular team or sport. They become bigger stars than ever, and they have an opportunity to make their professional careers last longer than if they were active only on the playing field.

Similar to the way agents are familiar with how to negotiate team contracts, they also help field and negotiate other marketing opportunities for the client. Some opportunities even go beyond the advertising field. Video games are another

AVERAGE ATHLETE SALARIES

If an athlete makes it to one of the four main professional leagues, his chances of being a millionaire for life increase dramatically. Although pro athletes don't play for many seasons in a row, their yearly salaries are quite impressive. Here are the average 2012 salaries of the athletes in the four main American professional sports leagues.

National Basketball Association: $5.15 million
Major League Baseball: $3.31 million
National Hockey League: $2.4 million
National Football League: $1.9 million

There are some professional athletes, like soccer player David Beckham, who make more money in product endorsements than they do playing sports.

big way to market professional athletes. Sports games such as football, soccer, and golf are popular among video game players. Some of these games feature the names and likenesses of real athletes and may even use their real voices in the games. A good agent will be able to find these opportunities, fight for their client to be part of the game, and then negotiate the price and even possible royalty share of the game sales.

Some pro athletes might have up to a dozen product endorsements or advertisements with their name or likeness on them. Product endorsement has become a popular way for athletes to gain exposure with the public as well as to make more money for themselves and their families to use after their on-the-field career has ended.

COMMUNICATING AND NETWORKING

With all that an agent does to help an athlete's career, you might wonder how all of the negotiating and deal making gets done. One very important aspect of a sports agent's job is to communicate and network with the people who will be giving his or her client contracts. With the average pro athlete's career lasting not much longer than four years, the agent is likely to carve a longer-lasting relationship with the team owners, advertising firms, media outlets, and public relations firms who deal with sports talents every day. Networking and keeping up good relationships with associates of all kinds can not only help with current contract negotiations but also indirectly affect future negotiations.

The most successful sports agents have a career-long reputation and a consistently good relationship with the people they do business with. A good reputation can take years to build and must be maintained constantly. But the agent with the best reputation will draw the most clients and will be able to negotiate the best rates for his or her clients.

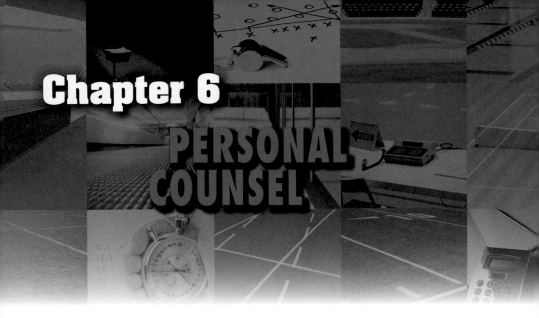

Chapter 6
PERSONAL COUNSEL

Professional athletes may sometimes need the help of lawyers beyond the negotiation of contracts for teams or commercial sponsorship. From time to time, some athletes may need help from personal counsel to assist them with legal issues. A personal counsel is a lawyer or a group of lawyers that will represent their client in court and present their case to the judge.

There are times when athletes may be involved in criminal matters, whether they are assumed to be the person who committed the crime or the person whom the crime is committed against.

In the case of Olympic athlete Oscar Pistorius, he was accused of murdering his girlfriend, model Reeva Steenkamp, on Valentine's Day, 2013. The woman was shot and killed through a bathroom door by Pistorius, but the South African double-amputee sprinter claimed that he thought the person on the other side of the door

Olympic athlete Oscar Pistorius *(left)* was in need of personal counsel while on trial for the murder of his girlfriend, Reeva Steenkamp.

was an intruder and that his actions were in defense of his home. A personal counsel is important in defending Pistorius. The actions of the personal counsel are extremely important in potentially keeping him out of jail as well as

helping to preserve his professional reputation.

Similarly, New England Patriots tight end Aaron Hernandez faced legal troubles when the body of a twenty-seven-year-old man was found in a wooded area about a mile from Hernandez's home. The job of Hernandez's legal counsel is to advise him on how to handle any charges against him and to help diffuse any unrelated, negative stories from affecting people's perception of the case. The legal counsel also represents the athlete to the media so that he does not have to talk to the media himself and possibly give any information that could affect the way his legal case is presented.

Personal counsel who represent athletes are not specialists in sports law. They specialize in presenting cases to a jury and judge, and they specialize in choosing jurors, collecting evidence, interviewing witnesses, and cross-examining witnesses in a courtroom setting. When the athlete is caught in a situation that affects his or her personal life and is unrelated to the athlete's career, a personal counsel is preferred over someone whose expertise is sports law. In other words, an athlete would not be wise to choose his or her agent as personal counsel, even though the agent has a degree in law. There are so many specialties in the law field that a person looking for a lawyer would be well advised to choose one that specializes in the particular kind of law he or she is looking for. For example, a sports agent would likely be out of practice in the courtroom. In some cases, it would be unlikely that a sports agent would have ever gained experience in the courtroom at all. Similarly, an athlete would likely not hire his or her personal counsel to negotiate contracts with teams or corporate sponsors.

Personal counsel may not only defend an athlete who is suspected of wrongdoing. A personal counsel may also press charges against someone else or request that the court place a particular legal order against someone. In 2011, tennis star Serena Williams went to court with personal counsel to request an order against someone she suspected was stalking her. Soon after, the man was arrested outside her home and charged with stalking and cyber-stalking.

While personal counsel may not specialize in sports, there are personal counsel who specialize in defending famous people, such as athletes. Most cases that involve people in the public eye will have a lot of media attention brought to them. Some counsel have a lot of experience defending people who are in the spotlight. These lawyers may be especially good at giving interviews to the media and at keeping the media away from their clients to prevent extra stress on the client or the client's family. They are comfortable defending high-profile clients and understand how to protect the assets of the client until the case is completely settled in a court of law.

However, a personal counsel cannot guarantee success for the client or return his or her reputation back to the way it was before the legal or scandalous incident. The public may retain its own opinions of the public personality, regardless of how the law sees the case or the person's actions.

PERSONAL IMAGE PROBLEMS

In some instances, a personal counsel can't help an athlete fix a personal image that has been tainted. In November 2009, news was released that superstar golfer Tiger Woods had an extramarital affair with a nightclub promoter. The adultery claims didn't end when nearly a dozen follow-up claims from other women caused Woods to lose his marital status as well as his $23 million worth of endorsements from sponsors such as Gillette, AT&T, General Motors, Gatorade, Nike, and Electronic Arts, the company that makes Tiger Woods video games. Woods is not the only one to have lost from the scandal. Many people work for the athlete in different capacities. His management company alone lost $4.6 million in its share of the athlete's earnings, and his managers lost $23 million. The star's personal problems even affected his game after he returned to it twenty weeks after the scandal. Once a confident winner of fourteen major championships such as the Masters Tournament, the U.S. Open, and the PGA Championships, the games after his scandal have not been as encouraging for fans, and he has lost his place as the world's best golfer.

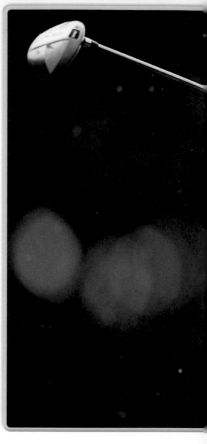

Former football quarterback Brett Favre's personal image was also badly damaged when texts with a female New York Jets employee were discovered. The scandal ruined his family-man image with the public and lost him his sponsorship with Wrangler jeans.

When an athlete must deal with personal setbacks in the eyes of the media, personal counsel may be the most helpful in working out compromises with sponsors or trying to keep the athlete out of the spotlight entirely. Tiger Woods's

Personal counsel attorney Mark NeJame guided star golfer Tiger Woods through difficult times in his personal life that caused him to lose many professional sponsorships, millions of dollars in endorsements, and his once-spotless public image.

personal attorney, Mark NeJame, represented the athlete and dealt with the media spotlight himself, going on many news programs and media outlets to discuss his client and to protect his privacy. He advised Woods and his family to decline all interviews and to remain out of the spotlight, even when the media made damaging statements about him.

PERFORMANCE-ENHANCING DRUG USE AND THE LAW

Some personal decisions athletes make have a direct effect on their game. For example, seven-time Tour de France winning cyclist Lance Armstrong, former world-champion track and field athlete and professional basketball player Marion Jones, and Major League Baseball players Barry Bonds and Roger Clemens were all accused of taking performance-enhancing drugs, which are strictly prohibited in professional sports.

The scandal involving Lance Armstrong was especially damaging to his career and his other professional endeavors. Armstrong was the founder and CEO of Livestrong, a cancer charity that the cancer survivor nurtured into a national symbol of cancer research and support. Armstrong lost $75 million in sponsorship deals. Even after admitting to "doping," his reputation had been ruined because of allegations from others about bullying them to keep quiet about the far-reaching scandal in the biking community. In addition to the lawsuits, Armstrong was banned for life from official sporting events and stripped of his seven Tour de France titles.

In the case of Lance Armstrong, he hired teams of lawyers to help protect him and his personal income in the face of the scandal. But lawyers are not cheap, especially at a time when someone is losing millions of dollars in

HIRING SPECIALTY LAWYERS

Most professional athletes will never see a courtroom due to their personal decisions or actions. However, with such high salaries, most professional athletes may need the help of a lawyer other than their agent now and then. Some athletes may have multiple homes and need the help of a real estate lawyer to look at contracts regarding the homes. Athletes may need help with legal matters regarding the purchase of a home, the sale of a home, and the transfer from one property to another.

An athlete will likely wish to write a last will and testament, which is a document that states what will happen to the athlete's money, real estate, and any other possessions after he or she dies.

There are many reasons for a personal counsel to help an athlete on a personal level. Choosing a lawyer with the right specialty will benefit the athlete above and beyond the need for a lawyer who specializes in sports law.

personal wealth. Facing at least six lawsuits against him, totaling more than $110 million, he had to gather the best personal defense lawyers that he could. This meant selling a home and downsizing his personal spending. But the experienced team of lawyers can only work within the law to help Armstrong regain any rights he lost due to his criminal activity. His reputation may be unable to

Scandal rocked the world of cycling when Lance Armstrong was charged with using performance-enhancing drugs. Armstrong required a team of lawyers to help him deal with problems that arose.

be improved no matter what the counsel may do for him financially or even professionally.

GAINING EXPERIENCE IN THE COURTROOM

To become a personal counsel who deals with high-profile cases such as those involving athletes, a lawyer may need decades of courtroom experience and a good, winning track record of successful cases.

While in law school, a person interested in criminal law should take as many classes about it as possible. This involves classes about the process of trying criminal cases, evidence, and what is allowed in courtrooms. It also involves reading about many cases in the past, how they were defended, and what the jury or judge decided in each case.

There are opportunities for law students to have either paid or unpaid positions as a clerk at a law firm or government agency. Clerks at either a public defender's office or a defense attorney's office can gain valuable experience in the entire courtroom process. Many law offices end up hiring the clerks that worked for them during law school, so the job of a clerk is a very important and valuable kind of internship program for students who are interested in criminal law.

As with other kinds of law, criminal lawyers and personal counsel lawyers use employees who do not have a

All kinds of law offices—from criminal lawyers, to personal counsel, to sports law specialists—require assistance from employees with varying levels of law training and education.

Juris Doctor degree. Legal secretaries, paralegals, and law associates can all help in researching, presenting, and defending a case in a courtroom. For example, a legal secretary would collect information vital to the case, such as paperwork or other documents that the defense or prosecution teams should have. The legal secretary would also prepare documents to file with the court and set and meet filing dates with the court about when paperwork should be complete and submitted to the court. Many of the legal secretary's duties are administrative and clerical. There is not much interaction with the client about the details of the case, although good phone, mail, and e-mail communication with the client is important. A legal secretary needs good computer and organizational skills, and good proofreading and editing skills are helpful when lawyers or other employees need to submit paperwork.

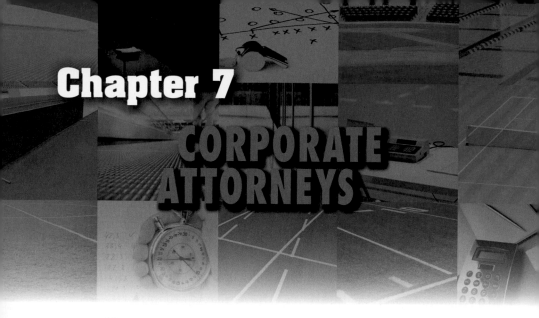

Chapter 7

CORPORATE ATTORNEYS

Corporations all around the world rely on the work of lawyers to help them set up and carry out their daily business. Depending on the type of business the corporation does, the common duties of the lawyer may vary. Companies that make sports equipment, manage sports games and performances, run stadiums, or make products that are endorsed by athletes may have a special working knowledge of sports law.

The world of a corporate lawyer may be much more social than that of a criminal attorney who works with clients in the courtroom. Corporations often have entire legal departments with many people working for them, both with law degrees and without. That creates a more traditional office environment than many other kinds of lawyers have. There may be a system of promotions in which people may rise in the company after gaining valuable experience on the job. Here are some of the things that corporate attorneys may be faced with, especially when the corporation relates to the world of sports.

KEEPING THE BUSINESS RUNNING

The job of any corporate lawyer would be to deal with all things legal. For example, the lawyers would make sure the company follows tax laws and submits proper financial reports. They make sure the company follows any rulebooks or codes of compliance for their industry regarding conduct or safety. They are involved in any large purchases the company makes or any mergers with other companies.

In more specific cases of companies that are related to the sports industry, corporate lawyers require more specialized knowledge that they may mainly get through on-the-job training.

ENSURING SAFE PRODUCTS

Companies such as Nike, Reebok, Adidas, Spalding, and Champion are engaged in fierce competition to put out quality sports equipment and apparel at affordable prices. Most important, however, their products must be safe for customers to use on a commercial level

Corporate lawyers are concerned that companies follow the law, present a good public image, and also make profits. Sporting goods companies are especially concerned with the safety of the products they sell or endorse.

as well as on a professional level.

Safety gear must pass safety standards. For example, two U.S. representatives in Congress released a bill that requires stronger standards for youth football helmets. The bill seeks to cut down on sports-related traumatic brain injuries in children. That means that the companies that make football helmets must respond. They now have a legal obligation to improve their product and ensure that it passes new safety standards. While lawyers are not involved in the designing or building of any new or improved helmets, the lawyers are involved in ensuring that the company has met its obligation in putting out products that comply with the

Sports gear made and sold by sporting goods companies must follow federal guidelines for safety. The companies must update their products when safety guidelines change.

safety standards and can be used legally by student football players on the field.

Lawyers also get involved in lawsuits against the company in cases of injury where an athlete blames the product for his or her injury. For example, companies that make bicycles may be faced with lawsuits against them if someone is injured or even killed riding one of their bikes. That does not necessarily mean that the sports equipment is faulty or unsafe. It simply means that the company must defend itself legally against the person's claims. Sometimes large companies try to keep cases out of the courtroom so that they do not attract negative media attention to their company or products. Corporate lawyers may meet with the person making the claim and settle the case out of court. Often that means that the company would offer money to the person who was injured or brought up the lawsuit. The money would be part of a legal agreement that may cover the person's medical expenses and possibly extra money for the troubles the situation caused the person and his or her family. Often, these types of settlements are done with contracts that state that the person will not sue the company for the incident again in the future and that he or she will keep the settlement confidential. That ensures the company that made the product that the case will not be brought up in the media. The reputations of corporations rest in the products they make and the way people are satisfied with those products.

SPORTING GOODS STORES

Sporting goods stores are especially concerned with the safety of their customers.

These stores deal mainly with amateur athletes who may get more easily injured using their products than professional athletes. The law departments of corpo-

Sporting goods stores protect themselves against lawsuits by providing safety information with products. They must also be concerned with issues such as safe displays, clearly marked merchandise, and sufficient room to move in the aisles.

rate sporting goods chains such as Modell's or Dick's Sporting Goods are also concerned with the safety of products that they sell. Instead of suing the company that made the store, injured customers may decide to sue the store that sold the product, claiming that they were not given enough information about it or that the sales associate sold them the wrong type of product. The legal departments of these companies are especially concerned with having employees learn about the products and deal with the public in a friendly and concerned matter, especially the managers.

In addition to helping the public stay safe when buying products, sporting goods stores are legally concerned with the safety of the store environment. Putting up safe displays is a top priority, especially when displaying heavy objects such as weights, bikes, or home gym equipment. Legal departments may put rules into place to help protect the public as well as the liability of the stores. That includes rules about where displays may be placed, how wide aisles in stores are, and how customers may get out of the stores carrying heavy equipment.

PROMOTIONS WITH THE PUBLIC

Many companies plan fun or elaborate giveaways for the public to help promote their company or product.

GETTING YOUR FOOT IN THE DOOR

Like other areas of law, a law student or other interested person can get a foot in the door of corporate law by applying for an internship or volunteer position while still in school. Companies that make sports equipment or apparel, teach sports, or are the actual sports teams, leagues, or stadiums themselves may offer internship opportunities to students. The internships may pay a small amount for travel expenses, or the internship program may offer only school credit. Volunteer or internship opportunities are a great way to make connections so that you can turn to someone later for a recommendation when you are looking for a job.

Sports companies are no exception. Legal departments become very involved in the detailed rules and regulations of public promotions. Legal regulations may be related to promotion dates, age requirements, or other restrictions. Some sports promotions may involve meeting a pro athlete or traveling on planes and staying in hotels. All of these things come with legal concerns in terms of safety and appropriate behavior on the part of the contest winner. Sometimes the contests simply involve free supplies or cash prizes. Legal concerns with these kinds of promotions have to do with the age of the contest winner and only allowing adults to enter the contest. In cases in which children can enter contests, legal teams are concerned with making sure the contestants have the permission of their parents or legal guardians. Each promotion can come with its own tricky legal concerns, so that is where corporate lawyers might come in. They can help ensure that the company does the right thing for the best interest of the public and the company's own reputation.

MEDIA CORPORATIONS

Large broadcasting companies such as ESPN, ABC, NBC, and CBS broadcast professional sports games and interview athletes. They are also large corporations with many lawyers looking out for the concerns of the broadcasting stations. First, there are many complex contracts involved in simply being allowed to broadcast the games and provide commentary for the public. Lawyers negotiate prices that the television stations would pay the sports leagues for each season or for a number of seasons.

In addition to the permission to broadcast games, a television station must have permission to interview athletes, coaches, managers, or owners. Some professional leagues may have special agreements with local television stations to get exclusive interview rights with their local teams.

The Internet has caused additional legal considerations when broadcasting games. Each of the main professional teams has its own Web site that broadcasts games, highlights, and interviews with athletes. These factors may affect the way that contracts are drafted with other broadcasters for a season. However, both the broadcasting station and the sports league are corporations. Lawyers in both places negotiate with each other and settle on the best agreement and the best price for both parties.

CONTRACTING WITH ATHLETES

Decades ago, the only business that a corporation would have with a professional athlete would be to contract that athlete to appear on a collectable trading card. Today, the world of sports is riddled with multimillion-dollar deals with athletes to sell products to the public. Many advertisements for companies such as Nike, Adidas, and Reebok feature all-star athletes. Even ads for non-sports products—such as razors, sodas, underwear, cars, watches, and airplanes—feature athletes. In fact, some athletes earn 80 to 95 percent of their money doing endorsements, not playing their sports. For example, tennis player Li Na earned 82 percent of her money from endorsements for companies such as Mercedes-Benz, Nike, Rolex, and Samsung. Soccer player David Beckham earned 89 percent of his money from endorsements for Armani, Samsung, Adidas, and his own underwear line for H&M

clothing stores. Tennis player Roger Federer earned 91 percent of his money from endorsements such as the ones he did for Gillette, Mercedes-Benz, and Nike. And track star Usain Bolt earned a staggering 99 percent of his total earnings from endorsements with companies such as Puma, Gatorade, and Virgin Media.

When a corporation signs an endorsement deal with an athlete, the corporation will usually place special wording in the contract to make sure that the star it has signed continues to live up to his or her reputation while the endorsement deal is in effect. That kind of clause is often a deal-breaker with the client. If the client does not agree to the clause, the

The image of a sports star is important to the corporations and institutions that athletes represent. Here, ESPN reporter Allison Williams interviews college basketball player Skylar Diggins after winning a game.

endorsement will not happen. But the clauses have proven to have serious implications for some bigger-than-life stars who got involved in personal and criminal trouble. Tiger Woods lost many of his corporate endorsements after his messy and public personal problems and divorce. Lance Armstrong also lost millions of dollars in corporate sponsorship when he admitted to taking performance-enhancing drugs during the time he won his seven Tour de France biking championships. Armstrong was stripped of the titles as well as $75 million in sponsorship deals.

A PROTECTIVE EYE

Another important part of corporate law is taking action when another company infringes on your company's copyrights or trademarks. For example, suppose a company comes out with swim goggles that have the same suction or no-leak feature that your company had trademarked. Legal teams would take on the mission of making sure the other company stopped selling the goggles and making a profit from the engineering or design that your company developed and has the sole legal right to. Corporate lawyers often find themselves in situations where they must defend trademarks or copyrights.

For example, a high-profile movie may decide to use your company's trademark, logo, or commercial jingle. If the moviemakers did not get permission from your company to use the reference, you may be in the position to sue them. There are many situations in films today in which products are placed in the background of a scene or an actor wears a hat or shirt from a sports team or product. These references are deliberately put into the movie as a kind of advertisement, or endorsement. If permission is not obtained, the film may be violating a copyright. Corporate lawyers are often on the lookout for these kinds of things, and the lawyers are often aggressive in their efforts to make sure the corporation is protected.

Corporate lawyers are often very competitive and aggressive in their work. If this kind of work is interesting to you and you think you have the personality for it, you may wish to consider corporate law, then search for work at a corporation that deals with sports, sports equipment, or professional athletes. As with all other areas of law, there are people who have a Juris Doctor degree and plenty who do not have the full law degree. Paralegals, law assistants, and legal secretaries work alongside lawyers to assist them. People with all levels of education can find a place in the field of sports law.

COLLEGE AND UNIVERSITY PROGRAMS IN LEGAL STUDIES

The following is a list of a number of colleges and universities that offer undergraduate programs in legal studies:

CUNY John Jay College of Criminal Justice
New York, New York
Programs of study: Legal studies

Illinois Institute of Technology
Chicago, Illinois
Programs of study: American/U.S. law/legal studies/jurisprudence, banking, corporate, finance, and securities law, legal research and advanced professional studies, legal studies, programs for foreign lawyers, tax law/taxation

Kaplan University
Davenport, Iowa
Programs of study: Legal administrative assistant, legal assistant/ paralegal, legal studies

St. John's University
Queens, New York
Programs of study: Securities law, legal studies, programs for foreign lawyers

University of California
Berkeley, California
Programs of study: Advanced legal, research studies, legal professions and studies, legal studies

University of California
Santa Barbara, California
Programs of study: Legal studies

University of Maryland—University College
Hyattsville, Maryland
Programs of study: Legal assistant/paralegal, legal studies

University of Massachusetts
Amherst, Massachusetts
Programs of study: Legal studies

University of Washington, Seattle Campus
Seattle, Washington
Programs of study: Legal research and advanced professional studies, tax law/taxation

University of Wisconsin
Madison, Wisconsin
Programs of study: Advanced legal studies, legal studies, research/studies

A CAREER IN SPORTS LAW AT A GLANCE

LAWYER/ATTORNEY

ACADEMICS

- Bachelor's degree
- LSAT exam
- Law school
- Bar exam

EXPERIENCE

- Internships at law firms or for district attorney's office

CAREER PATHS

- Lawyers specializing in sports can specialize in contract law.

- Some lawyers become sports agents and represent clients.

- Some lawyers specialize in making and enforcing regulations on the college and professional level.

DUTIES AND RESPONSIBILITIES

- Understand the law and explain it to clients

- Know how the law affects your clients

- Defend your clients and their legal rights

- Negotiate agreements between your client and other parties

PARALEGAL

ACADEMICS

- Associate's degree or bachelor's degree

- Take certified paralegal examination

- Work in legal field

- Take CLE (continuing legal education) courses or attend law school to become lawyer

EXPERIENCE

- Assisting lawyers in law offices or in court to gather and analyze documents and data

CAREER PATHS

- Paralegals specializing in sports law can assist lawyers in representing athletes, teams, or sports organizations.

- Some paralegals work in corporations, law offices, or courtrooms.

- Some paralegals communicate with clients about contracts or help lawyers negotiate terms of contracts.

- Some paralegals help enforce regulations at the college and professional level or analyze whether regulations have been violated.

DUTIES AND RESPONSIBILITIES

- Understand law and important law cases

- Present a professional attitude and atmo-sphere to client

- Assist lawyers in legal responsibilities with clients

LEGAL SECRETARY

ACADEMICS

- Completion of legal secretary certificate
- Possible associate's degree

EXPERIENCE

- Assisting lawyers prepare, file, and access legal documents

CAREER PATHS

- Legal secretaries specializing in sports law assist lawyers with documents related to athlete clients.

- Some legal secretaries work in corporations, law offices, or courtrooms.

- Some legal secretaries interact with clients by making appointments, taking notes in meetings, and providing clients with paperwork.

DUTIES AND RESPONSIBILITIES

- Present a professional attitude and atmosphere to clients and potential clients

- Perform detail-oriented tasks such as filing of hard copy and digital files, typing, writing letters, and taking accurate notes in legal meetings

- File legal documents with courts, government agencies, and corporations

SPORTS LAWYER

SIGNIFICANT POINTS

- Many lawyers work long, irregular hours.

- Acceptance to law school is highly competitive.

- The bar examination is very competitive, and some law graduates must take the bar exam several times before they pass.

NATURE OF THE WORK

Sports law can be a fast-paced, highly competitive field involving large amounts of money and high-profile clients. Many lawyers are known as being aggressive.

TRAINING

Formal requirements include a four-year bachelor degree, three years of law school, and passing a written examination called the bar examination.

OTHER QUALIFICATIONS

People who wish to be sports lawyers should know as much as possible about sports, especially any area of sports that they wish to work in. Sports lawyers know as much about sports as they do about the law, and they stay on top of changes in the sports industry, such as athlete trades from team to team and new product endorsements by athletes.

ADVANCEMENT

Some sports lawyers may advance by gaining experience in the field and adding new clients to their business. A good reputation can help a sports lawyer's business. Some sports lawyers start their own business or join a group business.

JOB OUTLOOK

Employment of sports lawyers is expected to grow 10 percent from 2010 to 2020, about as fast as the average for all occupations.

WORK ENVIRONMENT

Many lawyers work in a private or corporate legal office. Sports lawyers may work in specialty agencies. The majority of work is full-time, and many work long hours.

PARALEGAL

SIGNIFICANT POINTS

- Many paralegals work long, irregular hours.

- Paralegals have considerable training in the law, even though they do not have a law degree.

- Paralegals do a lot of work to assist lawyers in doing their job, such as maintaining and organizing files, conducting legal research, and drafting documents.

NATURE OF THE WORK

Sports law for a paralegal is usually similar to that of a lawyer. The work can be fast-paced and highly competitive, and involve large amounts of money and high-profile clients. Many paralegals do detailed or tedious work.

TRAINING

Most paralegals have an associate's degree or a certificate in paralegal studies. In some cases, employers may hire college graduates with a bachelor's degree and provide them with the necessary legal training on the job.

OTHER QUALIFICATIONS

People who wish to be paralegals must be prepared to do detailed work and pay special attention to how the law is interpreted by the lawyers they are working for. Paralegals interested in sports law should pay special attention to cases involving sports and the law, and learn as much as they can about sports and how it affects clients.

ADVANCEMENT

Paralegals may advance in their own law firm by assisting lawyers with higher standings or more clients. They may also move to firms with more prestigious or high-profile clients.

JOB OUTLOOK

Employment of paralegals is expected to grow 10 percent from 2010 to 2020, about as fast as the average for all occupations.

WORK ENVIRONMENT

Many paralegals work in private or corporate legal offices. Paralegals in sports law may work in specialty agencies. The majority of work is full-time, and many paralegals work long hours.

LEGAL SECRETARY

SIGNIFICANT POINTS

- Many legal secretaries work long hours but are not expected to work hours as long as lawyers or paralegals.

- Legal secretaries are trained in filling out and filing legal paperwork.

- Paralegals do a lot of work to assist lawyers, such as maintaining and organizing files, taking notes in legal meetings, drafting documents, and organizing legal files.

NATURE OF THE WORK

Work in law offices may be fast-paced and require quick and accurate responses from legal secretaries. They help with the day-to-day work, and their job is very important to the support of the firm.

TRAINING

Most legal secretaries have no more than an associate's degree and are not required to have an associate's degree to do the work. A legal secretary certificate is all that is needed for a legal secretary to work in most firms.

OTHER QUALIFICATIONS

Legal secretaries must be very detail-oriented and accurate in their work. They must take direction well and be professional in their demeanor.

ADVANCEMENT

Legal secretaries may advance by assisting lawyers with higher standings or more clients. They may also move to firms with more prestigious or high-profile clientele.

JOB OUTLOOK

Employment of legal secretaries is expected to grow 10 percent from 2010 to 2020, about as fast as the average for all occupations.

WORK ENVIRONMENT

Many legal secretaries work in private or corporate legal offices. Legal secretaries in sports law may work in specialty agencies. The majority of work is full-time.

agent A person who acts on behalf of another person or group, particularly in a legal matter.

associate's degree Post–high school level degree that usually requires two years of study.

bachelor's degree Post–high school level degree that usually requires four years of study.

bankruptcy The state of being unable to pay out-standing debts.

bar examination Test taken by graduates of law school to qualify them for studying law in a certain state or area.

bribe To persuade someone to act in a certain way, especially in an illegal or dishonest way, in exchange for a reward.

certificate Official document that attests that a certain level of achievement or study has been completed.

commissioner Person appointed to regulate a par-ticular sport.

compliance officer Person appointed to enforce rules and regulations in an official capacity.

contract A legal document that sets forth the terms of an agreement between two or more parties.

corruption Dishonest conduct by people in power, often involving bribery or favoritism.

Division I The highest level of three of college athletics as arranged by the National Collegiate Athletic Association (NCAA).

Division II The second highest level of three of college athletics as arranged by the National Collegiate Athletic Association (NCAA).

Division III The third level of three of college athletics as arranged by the National Collegiate Athletic Association (NCAA).

doping The process of administering drugs to an athlete in order to enhance the person's sporting performance.

endorsement The act of giving public approval or support to a product, cause, or idea.

ethical Related to moral principles and dealing with moral principles.

fine A sum of money that must be paid as a penalty for wrong behavior.

guideline A general rule or guiding principle.

internship An unpaid or low-paying entry level position that is meant for training purposes and may provide school credits.

Juris Doctor Professional college graduate degree that certifies that a person has completed law school.

legal secretary Person who assists lawyers in the legal profession.

lockout The exclusion of employees from their place of work until certain terms are agreed to.

LSAT Law School Admissions Test; a standardized test that is used to decide which students are admitted to law school.

marketing The action or business of promoting or selling products or services.

master's degree Academic, postgraduate degree.

mediation The intervention of a third party in a dispute in an attempt to solve the problem.

MLB Major League Baseball; professional men's baseball league in North America, consisting of the American League and National League.

NBA National Basketball Association; men's professional basketball league in North America.

NCAA National Collegiate Athletic Association; non-profit organization that organizes college-level athletics programs in the United States and Canada.

negotiation A discussion aimed at reaching an agreement between two or more parties.

NFL National Football League; professional American football league consisting of the National Football Conference and the American Football Conference.

NHL National Hockey League; association that controls the operations of thirty hockey teams throughout the United States and Canada.

paralegal A person trained in legal matters who is not a fully qualified lawyer.

penalty A punishment that results from a person or group breaking a rule, law, or contract.

personal counsel Professional services of a lawyer who can represent and defend a client in court.

public relations The professional attention to a company's or celebrity's public image.

recruit To enlist or enroll someone for a certain purpose.

referee An official who watches a sports game closely to ensure the rules are followed.

regulation Rule or directive made by a recognized leader or authority.

represent To act or speak on behalf of another person or entity.

restriction A condition that limits a person or group, especially in a legal sense.

scholarship Grant or payment of a student's education by another party.

settlement An official agreement meant to solve a dispute between parties.

terminate To end, especially in a legal sense.

violation The act of breaking a rule or formal agreement, or not complying with regulations.

FOR MORE INFORMATION

Canada National Olympic Committee
4141 Pier-de-Coubertin
Montreal, QC H1V 3N7
Canada
(514) 861-3371
Web site: http://olympic.ca
The Canada National Olympic Committee is an organization that tracks the Olympic records and activities of Canadian athletes participating in the Olympic Games.

Court of Arbitration for Sports (CAS)
North America: International Center for Dispute Resolution/American Arbitration Association
120 Broadway, 21st Floor
New York, NY 10271
(212) 716-3931
Web site: http://www.tas-cas.org
This agency takes care of any dispute arising from or in connection with the Olympic Games and solves the dispute in accordance with the Code of Sports-Related Arbitration.

International Sports Federations
Chateau de Vidy
Case postale 356
1001 Lausanne
Switzerland

Web site: http://www.olympic.org
This international, nonprofit agency monitors the way many
    international sports disciplines are recognized, regulated,
    and played.

National Collegiate Athletic Association
700 W. Washington Street
P.O. Box 6222
Indianapolis, IN 46206
(717) 917-6222
Web site: http://www.ncaa.org
This nonprofit organization promotes the academic and
    athletic achievement of college athletes, providing
    three divisions of play and regulations for play within
    each division.

National Sports Law Institute
P.O. Box 1881
Milwaukee, WI 53201
(414) 288-7090
Web site: http://law.marquette.edu/national-sports-law-institute
This organization is a national institute for education and
    research for the study of legal, ethical, and business
    issues that affect amateur and professional sports. Part
    of Marquette University Law School, law students are
    provided with opportunities to learn about and discuss
    sports law.

National Women's Law Center
11 Dupont Circle NW, #800
Washington, DC 20036
(202) 588-5180
Web site: http://www.nwlc.org
The National Women's Law Center is an organization that
    promotes opportunity and advancement for women and

girls in all aspects of their lives, including equality in sports and Title IX disputes.

Sport Business Research Network
P.O. Box 2378
Princeton, NJ 08543
(609) 896-1996
Web site: http://www.sbrnet.com
The organization assists individuals and organizations interested in sports-related issues, such as market research, government statistics, lawsuit records, and reports about sports facilities and venues.

Sports Lawyers Association (SLA)
12100 Sunset Hills Road
Suite 130
Reston, VA 20190
(703) 437-4377
Web site: http://www.sportslaw.org
The Sports Lawyers Association is a nonprofit, international professional organization dedicated to the understanding and advancement of ethics in sports law. It provides a forum for lawyers who represent athletes, teams, leagues, and conferences.

U.S. National Olympic Committee
1 Olympic Plaza
Colorado Springs, CO 80909
(719) 632-5551
Web site: http://www.teamusa.org
This organization tracks the Olympic records and activities of American athletes participating in the Olympic Games.

World Anti-Doping Agency
800 Place Victoria,

Suite 1700
P.O. Box 120
Montreal, QC H4Z 1B7
Canada
(514) 904-9232
Web site: http://www.wada-ama.org
The World Anti-Doping Agency promotes scientific
    research and education in anti-doping and monitors the
    World Anti-Doping Code that lays out anti-doping poli-
    cies in sports throughout the world.

WEB SITES

Due to the changing nature of Internet links, Rosen
Publishing has developed an online list of Web sites related
to the subject of this book. This site is updated regularly.
Please use this link to access the list:

http://www.rosenlinks.com/GCSI/Law

FOR FURTHER READING

Carfagna, Peter A. *Representing the Professional Athlete* (American Casebook). St. Paul, MN: West, 2009.

Champion, Walter T., Jr. *Sports Law in a Nutshell*. St. Paul, MN: Thompson/West, 2009.

Cozzillio, Michael J. *Sports Law: Cases and Materials*. Durham, NC: Carolina Academic Press, 2007.

Crasnick, Jerry. *License to Deal: A Season on the Run with a Maverick Baseball Agent*. Emmaus, PA: Rodale Books, 2005.

Dell, Donald. *Never Make the First Offer (Except When You Should): Wisdom from a Master Dealmaker*. New York, NY: Portfolio Hardcover, 2009.

Falk, David. *The Bald Truth: Secrets of Success from the Locker Room to the Boardroom*. New York, NY: Gallery Books, 2010.

Hatch, Scott, and Lisa Zimmer Hatch. *Paralegal Career for Dummies*. Hoboken, NJ: Wiley Publishing, 2011.

Pittman, Andrew, John O. Spengler, and Sarah Young. *Case Studies in Sport Law with Web Resource*. Champaign, IL: Human Kinetics, 2007.

Rosenhaus, Drew, and Jason Rosenhaus. *Next Question: An NFL Super Agent's Proven Game Plan for Business Success*. New York, NY: Berkley Trade, 2009.

Rosenhaus, Drew, and Don Yaeger. *A Shark Never Sleeps: Wheeling and Dealing with the NFL's Most Ruthless Agent*. New York, NY: Atria Books, 1998.

Saldana, Alfonso. *The Law and Paralegal Student's Guide to Legal Research and Writing.* Seattle, WA: Amazon Digital Services, 2012.

Schneider, Steven. *The Everything Guide to Being a Paralegal.* Avon, MA: Adams Media, 2006.

Sharp, Linda, Anita Moorman, and Cathryn Claussen. *Sport Law: A Managerial Approach.* 2nd ed. Scottsdale, AZ: Holcomb Hathaway, 2010.

Shropshire, Kenneth L. *Negotiate Like the Pros: A Top Sports Negotiator's Lessons for Making Deals, Building Relationships, and Getting What You Want.* New York, NY: McGraw-Hill, 2008.

Shropshire, Kenneth L, and Timothy Davis. *The Business of Sports Agents.* Philadelphia, PA: University of Pennsylvania Press, 2008.

Spengler, John O., Paul Anderson, Dan Connaughton, and Thomas Baker. *Introduction to Sport Law.* Champaign, IL: Human Kinetics, 2009

Stein, Mel. *How to Be a Sports Agent.* New York, NY: Oldcastle Books, 2012.

Thorton, Patrick K. *Sports Law.* Sudbury, MA: Jones & Bartlett Publishers, 2010.

Wells, Michelle, Andy Kreutzer, and Jim Kahler. *A Career in Sports: Advice from Sports Business Leaders.* Livonia, MI: M. Wells Enterprises, 2010.

Wong, Glenn M. *The Comprehensive Guide to Careers in Sports.* Burlington, MA: Jones and Bartlett Learning, 2012.

Wong, Glenn M. *Essentials of Sports Law.* New York, NY: Praeger, 2010.

BIBLIOGRAPHY

Angst, Frank. "Sports Business Journal a Favorite of Sports Executives." About.com. Retrieved July 9, 2013 (http://sportscareers.about.com/od/otherresources/a/SBJprofile.htm).

Aschburner, Steve. "NBA's 'Average' Salary—$5.15M—A Trendy, Touchy Subject." NBA.com, August 19, 2011. Retrieved July 11, 2013 (http://www.nba.com/2011/news/features/steve_aschburner/08/19/average-salary/index.html).

Associated Press. "Lance Armstrong Shamed by Doping Scandal." Foxnews.com, January 19, 2013. Retrieved July 14, 2013 (http://www.foxnews.com/sports/2013/01/19/lance-armstrong-shamed-by-doping-scandal).

BaseballStadiums.net. "Baseball Stadiums." Retrieved July 11, 2013 (http://www.baseballstadiums.net).

Brady, Erik. "Who Is the Most Disliked Commissioner in Sports?" *USA Today*, September, 27, 2012. Retrieved July 9, 2013 (http://usatoday30.usatoday.com/sports/story/2012/09/27/who-is-the-most-disliked-commissioner-in-sports/57849516/1).

Brady, Tom, and Drew Brees. "Injured Pro Athletes Deserve Workers' Comp." *San Francisco Chronicle*, June 24, 2013. Retrieved July 20, 2013 (http://www.sfchronicle.com/opinion/openforum/article/Injured-pro-athletes-deserve-workers-comp-4617644.php).

BrooWaha.com. "NFL Primer: Exactly What Does the NFL Commissioner Do?" November 10, 2010.

Retrieved July 12, 2013 (http://www.broowaha.com/ articles/8490/nfl-primer-exactly-what-does-the-nfl -commissioner-do).

Brumfield, Ben. "Blade Runner Oscar Pistorius, Awaiting Murder Trial, Sprints Again." CNN.com, June 28, 2013. Retrieved July 20, 2013 (http://www.cnn .com/2013/06/28/world/africa/south-africa -pistorius).

Campus Explorer. "Top 10 Most Popular Legal Studies Colleges." Retrieved July 2013 (http://www .campusexplorer.com/colleges/major/E8533CC3/ Legal-Professions/0D8A4E2F/Legal-Studies).

College Sports Scholarships.com. "Athletic Divisions of the NCAA: Colleges Have to Meet Certain Standards to Compete in Each Division." Retrieved July 6, 2013 (http://www.collegesportsscholarships.com/ ncaa-divisions-differences.htm).

DegreeDictionary.org. "What Does a Legal Secretary Do?" Retrieved July 17, 2013 (http://degreedirectory.org/ articles/What_Does_a_Legal_Secretary_Do.html).

DeLuca, Matthew. "Body Found Near Patriots Player Aaron Hernandez's Home Ruled a Homicide." NBC News.com, June 20, 2013. Retrieved July 19, 2013 (http://usnews.nbcnews.com/_ news/2013/06/20/19058232-body-found -near-patriots-player-aaron-hernandezs-home -ruled-a-homicide?lite).

DiscoverLaw.org. "Law School Basics." Retrieved July 17, 2013 (http://www.discoverlaw.org/considering/law- school-basics.asp).

Dorish, Joe. "Average Salaries in the NBA, NFL, MLB, and NHL." Yahoo Sports, November 12, 2011. Retrieved July 15, 2013 (http://sports.yahoo.com/ nba/news?slug=ycn-10423863).

Dunbar, Graham. "Lance Armstrong Stripped of His 7 Tour de France Titles." WWLT.com, October 22, 2012. Retrieved July 18, 2013 (http://www.wwltv .com/sports/UCI-agrees-to-stripping-Armstrong -of-Tour-de-France-medals-175217311.html).

Federal Mediation & Conciliation Service. "Deputy Director Scot L. Beckenbaugh: Biographical Information." Retrieved July 7, 2013 (http://www .fmcs.gov/internet/itemDetail.asp?categoryID= 93&itemID=19004).

Field, Shelly. *Career Opportunities in the Sports Industry.* New York, NY: Checkmark Books, 2004.

Fortenbaugh, Joe. "Ranking the NFL Stadiums: Where Does Your Team Fall Among the 31 Venues?" February 17, 2011. Retrieved July 3, 2013 (http:// www.nationalfootballpost.com/Ranking-the-NFL -Stadiums.html).

Geiger Smith, Erin. "Tiger Woods' Lawyer Mark NeJame: Who Is He?" Business Insider, November 30, 2009. Retrieved July 20, 2013 (http://www.businessinsider .com/tiger-woods-lawyer-mark-nejame-who-is -he-2009-11).

Golden, Geoffrey. "How Much Has Tiger Woods Lost in Endorsements?" Celebrity Networth.com, August 11, 2012. Retrieved July 17, 2013 (http://www .celebritynetworth.com/articles/entertainment -articles/how-much-has-tiger-woods-lost -in-endorsements/).

Hackney Publications. "Legal Issues in High School Athletics." Retrieved July 8, 2013 (http://www. hackneypublications.com/lihsa/issues/2009/LIHSA- 2009-July-August.php).

Herrmann, Mark. "Hideki Matsui Honored at Yankee Stadium After Signing One Day Contract, Retiring."

Long Island Newsday, July 28, 2013. Retrieved November 30, 2013. (http://www.newsday.com/sports/baseball/yankees/hideki-matsui-honored-at-yankee-stadium-after-signing-one-day-contract-retiring-1.5784691).

Hyman, Jeremy S., and Lynn F. Jacobs. "10 Tips for Starting Your College Search." USNews.com, December 30, 2009. Retrieved July 20, 2013, (http://www.usnews.com/education/blogs/professors-guide/2009/12/30/10-tips-for-starting-your-college-search).

Investopedia. "Top 4 TV Sports Deals of 2011." September 23, 2011. Retrieved July 14, 2013 (http://www.investopedia.com/financial-edge/0911/top-4-tv-sports-deals-of-2011.aspx).

Jobs in Sports. "Sports Law Jobs & Internships." Retrieved July 2, 2013 (http://www.jobsinsports.com/sports-law-jobs.cfm).

Johnson, Philip. "18 Athletes Who Make More Money Endorsing Products Than Playing Sports." Business Insider, June 6, 2013. Retrieved July 20, 2013 (http://www.businessinsider.com/18-athletes-more-money-endorse-sport-2013-6?op=1).

Kaplan University. "Bachelor of Science in Legal Studies." Retrieved July 3, 2013 (http://www.kaplanuniversity.edu/legal-studies/legal-studies-bachelor-degree.aspx).

Kaplan University. "Bachelor of Science in Paralegal Studies." Retrieved July 3, 2013 (http://www.kaplanuniversity.edu/legal-studies/paralegal-studies-bachelor-.aspx).

Kaplan University. "Legal Secretary Certificate." Retrieved July 3, 2013 (http://www.kaplanuniversity.edu/legal-studies/legal-secretary-certificate.aspx).

Klicka, Chris. "Can Homeschoolers Participate in Public School Programs?" Homeschool World. Retrieved

July 14, 2013 (http://www.home-school.com/Articles/
can-homeschoolers-participate-in-public-school
-programs.php).

Lubinger, Bill. "Violation or Legal? Do You Have What
It Takes to Be an NCAA Compliance Officer? Here's
Your Shot." Cleveland.com, June 9, 2011. Retrieved
July 14, 2013 (http://www.cleveland.com/osu/index.
ssf/2011/06/violation_or_legal_do_you_have.html).

Mail Online. "Serena Williams' Stalker Arrested Outside Her
Florida Home While She Attended the Met Gala." May 3,
2011. Retrieved July 18, 2013 (http://www.dailymail.co.uk/
tvshowbiz/article-1383239/Serena-Williams-stalker
-busted-outside-Florida-home-attended-Met-Gala.html).

National Collegiate Athletic Association. "Eligibility:
Fairness. Academics. Equitable Competition."
Retrieved July 3, 2013 (http://www.ncaa.org/wps/
wcm/connect/public/ncaa/eligibility/index.html).

Newcomer, Lara. "20 Sports Equipment Companies That
Do Good." Greatist.com, October 5, 2012. Retrieved
November 30, 2013. (http://greatist.com/fitness/
social-good-sports-equipment-companies).

NFL.com. "Fines in 2012: ($2,873,075)." Retrieved July 7,
2013 (http://justfines.com/listFines.php?year=2012).

NFL.com. "Rule Book: Digest of Rules." Retrieved July 7,
2013 (http://www.nfl.com/rulebook/digestofrules).

Pascrell, Bill. "Rep. Pascrell, Sen. Udall Introduce
Legislation Requiring Stronger Standards for Youth
Football Helmets." Press Release, March 16, 2011.
Retrieved July 17, 2013 (http://pascrell.house.gov/
list/press/nj09_pascrell/pr031620112.shtml).

Podell, Ira. "NHL Lockout 2012: Mediator Gets League,
Union Back Together." *Washington Times*, January 5,
2013. Retrieved July 17, 2013 (http://www
.washingtontimes.com/news/2013/jan/5/nhl

-lockout-2012-mediator-gets-league-union
-back-t/?page=all).

Ritz, Erica. "Mom Upset After Christian School Tells
Girl She Can't Play Football on the Boy's Team
Anymore...and Allegedly Cites the Bible to Justify
It." The Blaze, June 24, 2013. Retrieved July 15, 2013
(http://www.theblaze.com/stories/2013/06/24/
mom-upset-after-christian-school-tells-girl-she
-cant-play-football-on-the-boys-team-anymore
-and-allegedly-cites-the-bible-to-justify-it).

Schrotenboer, Brent. "Amid Lawsuits and Lost Income,
Lance Armstrong Downsizes." USA Today, April
12, 2013. Retrieved July 17, 2013 (http://www
.usatoday.com/story/sports/cycling/2013/04/11/
lance-armstrong-downsizes/2075907).

Sports Illustrated. "SI's 50 Most Powerful People in
Sports." Retrieved July 12, 2013 (http://
sportsillustrated.cnn.com/main/photos/1303/
50-most-powerful-people-in-sports/5).

The Sports Xchange. "NFL to Enforce Rules Against
Coaches Stepping onto Field During Game." Yahoo
Sports, February 20, 2013. Retrieved July 20, 2013
(http://sports.yahoo.com/news/nfl-enforce-rules
-against-coaches-025128891—nfl.html).

Superpages.com. "What Does a Corporate Lawyer Do?"
Retrieved July 20, 2013 (http://www.superpages
.com/supertips/corporate-lawyer.html).

Time. "A Brief History of the Tiger Woods Scandal."
Retrieved July 7, 2013 (http://www.time.com/time/
photogallery/0,29307,1966486,00.html).

Tuttle, Brad. "NHL Lockout Is Over! Guess Who's
Happier Than Fans or Players?" Time, January 8,
2013. Retrieved July 9, 2013 (http://business.time
.com/2013/01/08/nhl-lockout-is-over-guess-whos
-happier-than-fans-or-players).

U.S. Department of Labor. "Title IX, Education Amendments of 1972." Retrieved July 5, 2013 (http://www.dol.gov/oasam/regs/statutes/titleix.htm).

WikiHow.com. "How to Become a Criminal Defense Lawyer." Retrieved July 20, 2013 (http://www.wikihow.com/Become-a-Criminal-Defense-Lawyer).

Wisegeek.com. "What Does a Sports Agent Do?" Retrieved July 12, 2013 (http://www.wisegeek.org/what-does-a-sports-agent-do.htm).

Wong, Glenn M. *The Comprehensive Guide to Careers in Sports*. Burlington, MA: Jones & Bartlett Learning, 2013.

INDEX

A

accounting, 66, 68
Adidas, 87, 97
advertising, 12, 43, 47, 55, 62, 64,
    68–72, 73, 87, 97–98, 100, 101
Anheuser-Busch, 16
Armani, 97
Armstrong, Lance, 80–83, 100
associate's degrees, 31, 32, 33, 67,
    105, 107, 111, 113
Athletic Business, 23
AT&T, 77

B

bachelor's degrees, 29, 31, 32, 33,
    67, 104, 105, 109, 111
bar exams, 30
Beckenbaugh, Scot, 53
Beckham, David, 97–98
Bettman, Gary, 53
Bolt, Usain, 98
Bonds, Barry, 80
Brady, Tom, 66
Brees, Drew, 66
bribes, 43, 44, 46
broadcasters, 55, 57, 62, 96–97
Bureau of Labor Statistics (BLS),
    109–115

C

certification, 30, 31, 67, 107, 111, 114
Champion, 87
Clemens, Roger, 80
coaches, 34, 36, 38, 41, 42, 44, 46,
    50, 52, 54, 56, 96
Coca-Cola, 16
commissioner's office, 47–58, 60
compliance officers, 27, 42–46
concessions, 14, 16–17
copyrights, 100–101
corporate attorneys, 86–101
Cruise, Tom, 67

D

Daly, Bill, 53
Denver Broncos, 13
Dick's Sporting Goods, 94
doping, 80

E

Education Amendments of
    1972, 36
Electronic Arts, 77
endorsements, 12, 13, 47, 64, 68, 71,
    77, 86, 97–98, 100–101, 110
ESPN, 55, 96

F

Facebook, 45
Favre, Brett, 78
Federer, Roger, 98
Frito-Lay, 16

G

Gatorade, 77, 98
General Motors, 77
Gillette, 77, 98
Goodell, Roger, 54–55, 58
Gooding, Cuba, Jr., 67

H

Hernandez, Aaron, 75
H&M, 97–98

I

Indiana High School Athletic
    Association, 36
informational interviews, 27–28
internships, 24, 26, 27, 29, 83, 95
interview tips, 29

J

Jerry Maguire, 67
job interviews, 29
Jones, Marion, 80
Juris Doctor (JD) degrees, 29, 30,
    33, 59, 85, 101

L

law assistants, 17, 20, 101
law clerks, 83

legal secretaries, 20, 30–31, 85,
    101, 107–108, 113–114
legal studies, college and
    university programs in,
    102–103
Li Na, 97
Little League, 24
Livestrong, 80
lockouts, 53–55
LSAT, 29, 30, 104

M

Major League Baseball (MLB),
    14, 24, 58, 70, 80
Manning, Peyton, 13
master's degrees, 33
Masters Tournament, 78
memorabilia, 13
mentoring, 27
Mercedes Benz, 97, 98
Modell's, 94
Monroe County Community
    School Corporation, 36–37

N

National Basketball Association
    (NBA), 13, 58, 62, 70
National Collegiate Athletic
    Association (NCAA), 27–28,
    40, 41–42, 43, 44
National Federation of State
    High School Associations
    (NFHS), 34
National Football League (NFL),
    50, 51, 52, 54–55, 57, 62, 70

National Hockey League (NHL), 53, 70
NeJame, Mark, 79
New England Patriots, 75
New York Jets, 78
Nielsen Research Group, 56–57
Nike, 64, 77, 87, 97, 98

O

Olympics, 73
online courses, 32
on-the-job training, 42, 67, 87
Oscar Meyer, 16

P

paralegals, 20, 32, 33, 58, 67, 85, 101, 105–106, 111–112
performance-enhancing drugs, 80
personal counsel, 73–85
PGA Championships, 78
Pistorius, Oscar, 73–75
player lockouts, 53–54
public promotions, 94–96
Puma, 98

R

recruiters, 5, 39, 44, 59
Reebok, 87, 97
referee lockouts, 54–55
Rolex, 97
royalty shares, 71
rulebooks, 42, 51, 87

S

safe products, ensuring, 87–92
salaries, 12, 13, 30, 48, 60, 62–64, 70, 81
Samsung, 97
scholarships, 6, 19, 39, 40, 41
school, choosing the right, 32
Selig, Bud, 58
social networking, 44–45
Spalding, 87
sponsors, 43, 47, 73, 76, 77, 78, 80, 100
sporting goods stores, 92–94
sports agents, 6, 59–72, 76, 81, 105
SportsBusiness Journal, 22
Sports Illustrated, 22
sports law, careers in,
    at a glance, 104–108
    BLS information, 109–115
    high school and college levels, 34–46
    overview of, 4–20
    preparing for, 21–33
stadiums, 8, 13–17, 55, 56, 64, 86, 95
Stanley Cup, 13
Steenkamp, Reeva, 73
Stern, David, 58
Super Bowl, 13, 47, 56–57

T

tax laws, 87
Title IX, 36, 37

Tour de France, 80, 100
trademarks, 100–101

U

umpires, 50
Univision, 55
U.S. Department of Labor, 36
U.S. Open, 78

V

video games, 70–71, 77
Virgin Media, 98
volunteering, 24–27, 29, 95

W

Williams, Serena, 76
Woods, Tiger, 77–78, 79, 100
World Cup, 55
World Series, 13, 47
Wrangler, 78

Y

Yahoo!, 57
Young, Logan, 36–38

ABOUT THE AUTHOR

Kathy Furgang has been writing educational books for teens for many years. She has written books about volunteer and internship programs in various professions. She also writes for teacher guides and textbooks for students in elementary and middle school.

PHOTO CREDITS